HAPPINESS FIRST

THE HEALTHY WAY TO ACADEMIC SUCCESS

PRADEEP R. BIJWE

Copyright © PRADEEP R. BIJWE
All Rights Reserved.

This book has been self-published with all reasonable efforts taken to make the material error-free by the author. No part of this book shall be used, reproduced in any manner whatsoever without written permission from the author, except in the case of brief quotations embodied in critical articles and reviews.

The Author of this book is solely responsible and liable for its content including but not limited to the views, representations, descriptions, statements, information, opinions and references ["Content"]. The Content of this book shall not constitute or be construed or deemed to reflect the opinion or expression of the Publisher or Editor. Neither the Publisher nor Editor endorse or approve the Content of this book or guarantee the reliability, accuracy or completeness of the Content published herein and do not make any representations or warranties of any kind, express or implied, including but not limited to the implied warranties of merchantability, fitness for a particular purpose. The Publisher and Editor shall not be liable whatsoever for any errors, omissions, whether such errors or omissions result from negligence, accident, or any other cause or claims for loss or damages of any kind, including without limitation, indirect or consequential loss or damage arising out of use, inability to use, or about the reliability, accuracy or sufficiency of the information contained in this book.

Made with ♥ on the Notion Press Platform
www.notionpress.com

I dedicate this book with immense reverence to my Guru,
Shri Bramhachaitanya Gondavalekar Maharaj
(1869-1913), whose simple yet profound teachings have
illuminated my path in the past 42 years.

Contents

Introduction

"Happiness is the meaning and the purpose of life, the whole aim and end of human existence." - Aristotle

Having studied at I.I.T. Delhi for five years and taught there for thirty-nine years, I recognized the importance of peace of mind during my postgraduate days. In my late twenties, I was fortunate to discover a spiritual path that profoundly influenced my professional and personal life. Throughout my years of interacting with students, I became acutely aware of their stress levels. It prompted me to explore ways to bring more happiness into their lives. I revisited my experiences as a student and observed the habits of exceptional students who consistently outperformed expectations despite not being the brightest. I also delved into numerous self-help books to gain further insights. In 2014, I introduced my ideas for a "happy student life" during a lecture for approximately five hundred first-year B. Tech students. The response was overwhelmingly positive and immediate. I created a "Joyful Living" web page to reach more students. Using the insights from these topics, I extended counseling services to students experiencing unhappiness for various reasons. This endeavor granted me valuable insights into students' diverse challenges and practical strategies to conquer them. Part II of the book includes the experiences of some students who could improve their lot through this exercise. However, due to the limited reach of these activities, I felt compelled to write a book that could touch a much larger audience. While colleges provide education for earning a livelihood, they often neglect to offer life education. To the best of my knowledge, no specific book is available for the students on the latter subject. While my experience is primarily based on my time at I.I.T. Delhi, most of the content in this book applies to students from any college and discipline.

Our purpose in life is to find happiness in every moment. However, it's no secret that college students everywhere are stressed. It applies to low- and top-tier college students, regardless of their academic abilities. While the specific reasons for stress may vary, it is unfortunately considered a normal part of the college experience. We often advise students to endure short-term pain for long-term gain. Still, this approach tends to result in a continuous cycle of arduous struggles followed by brief moments of joy upon achieving milestones.

We all strive for success and happiness, yet we only fleetingly achieve these states. Some may possess extreme wealth, fame, or power, but nearly everyone fears losing these external factors and, as a result, remains unhappy. Hence, our understanding of true success and happiness is flawed. We constantly feel stressed, worried, and anxious because we instinctively know that outcomes may not meet our expectations. Numerous factors beyond our control influence the results we desire. This stress prevents us from focusing on the process and doing our best. If we examine interviews with accomplished individuals from various fields, we will notice a common theme: they emphasize the importance of enjoying the process and not fixating on the outcome. This mind-set sets them up for success more often. Additionally, failures may occur, but their open-mindedness allows them to learn from those experiences and move forward without losing morale. This book delves into this approach, where success lies in doing our best rather than simply achieving the best results.

In this alternative and healthier approach, it is crucial to cultivate inner peace and happiness. We also require intelligent and effective work practices in the external world. However, the former is paramount to the success of the latter.

We must prioritize our physical and mental well-being to achieve success and enjoy life. While most of us recognize the importance of physical health, understanding mental health is often lacking. Neglecting this vital aspect is the cause of much suffering. We acknowledge that production equipment must be maintained to produce quality output consistently. Yet, we often forget that we, as humans, are the most complex entities on Earth. We have been utilizing this incredible machinery without truly understanding even its basics. As a result, most of us operate well below our physical and mental capabilities, often without even realizing it. We don't need the physical fitness levels of athletes or the mind control of yogis. Simple, time-efficient practices are sufficient to enhance our happiness and work efficiency significantly. Our minds and brains are remarkable gifts, but many of us are unaware of their functioning and that they can be improved through lifelong self-learning. With simple exercises, we can unlock our untapped potential.

In groundbreaking research, positive psychologists led by Martin Seligman studied how certain individuals thrived in the most adverse situations. They discovered that practicing happiness improves one's chances of success. Through their extensive studies at Harvard, Tal Ben-Shahar and Shawn Achor have explored and written books on this approach [1, 2].

Many books advocate for pursuing our passions to find happiness. However, most of us are not passionate about studying, and we also must engage in numerous daily routines and mundane tasks. If we are unhappy while performing these tasks, we will suffer daily. This is why the following approach is more practical:

Mother Teresa once said, *"Not all of us can do great things. But we can do small things with great love."* We can only perform tasks with love when we are happy. At first glance, this may seem like a "chicken or egg" dilemma. However, researchers have shown that practicing happiness provides a way out. This book demonstrates how to navigate this path.

We all know that we perform better when we are at peace rather than under stress, whether in our studies, exams, interviews, sports, jobs, or even relationships. Achieving inner peace and harmony is possible only when we cultivate a love for ourselves, other human beings, our work, and the environment. This book shows how this approach is crucial for student success.

Yogis developed meditation techniques thousands of years ago to control breathing and attain peace and happiness by observing the connection between our emotional state and breathing. Chade-Meng Tan, a former Google engineer, has popularized these techniques through his "Search Inside Yourself" program and books, demonstrating their effectiveness in enhancing emotional intelligence and happiness [3, 4]. Doctors, psychologists, and researchers have also found that mindfulness meditation has incredible utility in improving work efficiency and nearly all aspects of our lives. Neurologists have confirmed that meditation enhances brain function and promotes the rewiring of neurons [5].

In practical life, we must practice what we wish to improve. To maintain lasting physical fitness, we must exercise consistently throughout our lives. Therefore, instead of waiting for fleeting moments of happiness, a proactive approach is to make happiness a habit through dedicated practice. Happiness brings smiles, laughter, slower breathing, natural gratitude, and positive thinking. These are the effects of happiness, which is the cause. Fortunately, research has proven these are bilateral processes between cause and effect. Hence, deliberately practicing each of these effects can bring us happiness. Throughout the day, we can incorporate happiness boosters into our lives by meditating, taking mindful deep breaths, offering prayers for well-being, expressing love for ourselves, others, our work, and our environment, showing gratitude, recalling positive experiences, smiling, and laughing whenever possible. These small acts are entirely within our control and provide immediate improvements in mood. Shawn Achor, the author of "The Happiness Advantage" [2], states, *"Waiting to be happy limits our brain's potential for success, whereas cultivating positive brains makes us more motivated, efficient, resilient, creative, and productive, which drives performance."* Therefore, practicing happiness develops the qualities necessary for success automatically.

Understanding what is necessary for success in college is not rocket science. Students know that attending classes regularly, studying consistently, improving sleep patterns, and effective time management are crucial for success. However, it is essential to understand why many struggle to implement these practices. In Indian mythology, an important character, Duryodhana, famously said, "I know what is good, but I have no inclination to act on it. I know what is bad, but I can't stop doing it." This sentiment encapsulates the dilemma faced by most of us. Many believe we are born with inherent physical, mental, and intellectual capabilities and limitations that cannot be significantly changed. This book challenges that notion and demonstrates that we can transform ourselves and improve our happiness and success.

Nick Vujicic was born without limbs, Helen Keller was deaf, dumb, and blind from a young age, and William James, the father of modern psychology, was a sickly weakling in a wealthy family who once contemplated suicide. However, through their choices and attitudes, they achieved happiness and became inspirations to the world. Viktor Frankl, the author of "Man's Search for Meaning," who survived years in a German concentration camp during World War II, stated, *"When we are no longer able to change a situation, we are challenged to change ourselves."* He also said, *"Everything can be taken away from a man but one thing: the last of the human freedoms - to choose one's attitude in any given set of circumstances."* We must apply this principle to face daily challenges [6].

The main motivation behind this book is to instil confidence in every student that improvement in success is indeed possible. It presents an unconventional approach of daily happiness practice for the same. This approach generates enthusiasm because the qualities necessary for success improve almost effortlessly.

Happiness is the most valuable skill to learn in life. This book introduces simple steps for cultivating happiness. Learning this skill is a lifelong journey that requires dedicated practice. However, taking the first few steps is easy and does not require much time. Achieving success during these initial steps will create momentum to keep you going. I have practiced these techniques for a long time and have immensely benefitted from them.

The book is divided into two parts. The first part introduces principles and practical strategies for happiness and success. The second part focuses on strategies to improve academic performance. The number of chapters may appear to be large; however, these are quite short and focussed.

The book's first part begins with understanding different types of happiness and their limitations so that we can choose wisely. It emphasizes enjoyment of the journey and not just fixating on the destination. It explains that loving ourselves unconditionally is essential for healthy self-esteem, a prerequisite for happiness. It shows that loving others, situations, work, and the environment is also important for happiness. It explains how to control our minds by changing our thoughts, beliefs, and values to positive ones. The benefits of meditation and mindfulness in improving our emotional intelligence and many other important qualities essential for happiness are also discussed. The importance of self-awareness about our aspirations, fears, emotions, and habits in improving our lives is discussed next. The power of prayers for improving our well-being and reducing our stress through a dialogue with a higher power is also explained. Likewise, how affirmations are powerful in mind reconditioning to a positive one is also discussed. Based on the above, simple and time-efficient daily practices are suggested to improve our happiness and success.

The book's second part utilizes the concepts in the first part for improved efficiency. To begin with, it discusses the right attitude for academics. It then shows how effective time management can be done to be successful. It provides tips for getting the best out of the integrated study components for success. Since most of the students in research-based degree programs do not understand the complexities of their work, a comprehensive discussion about all the aspects is discussed, which is rarely found anywhere. The book also discusses how to bounce back after setbacks and provides real-life examples of people who did that. Finally, the book discusses how best to prepare for the future right from the first year, considering individual aspirations and the uncertainties involved.

To achieve measurable results from this book, adapt the ideas in this book to your specific circumstances. I suggest highlighting and taking notes as you read, which will help you focus. Then, create an action plan to implement the concepts in your life. Start with just a few ideas and observe how they make you feel. If they bring you joy, gradually incorporate more practices into your routine. Consider this book your operating manual - refer to it repeatedly, as it will assist you in your academic, professional, and personal journey.

I love you and wish you all the best for your journey.

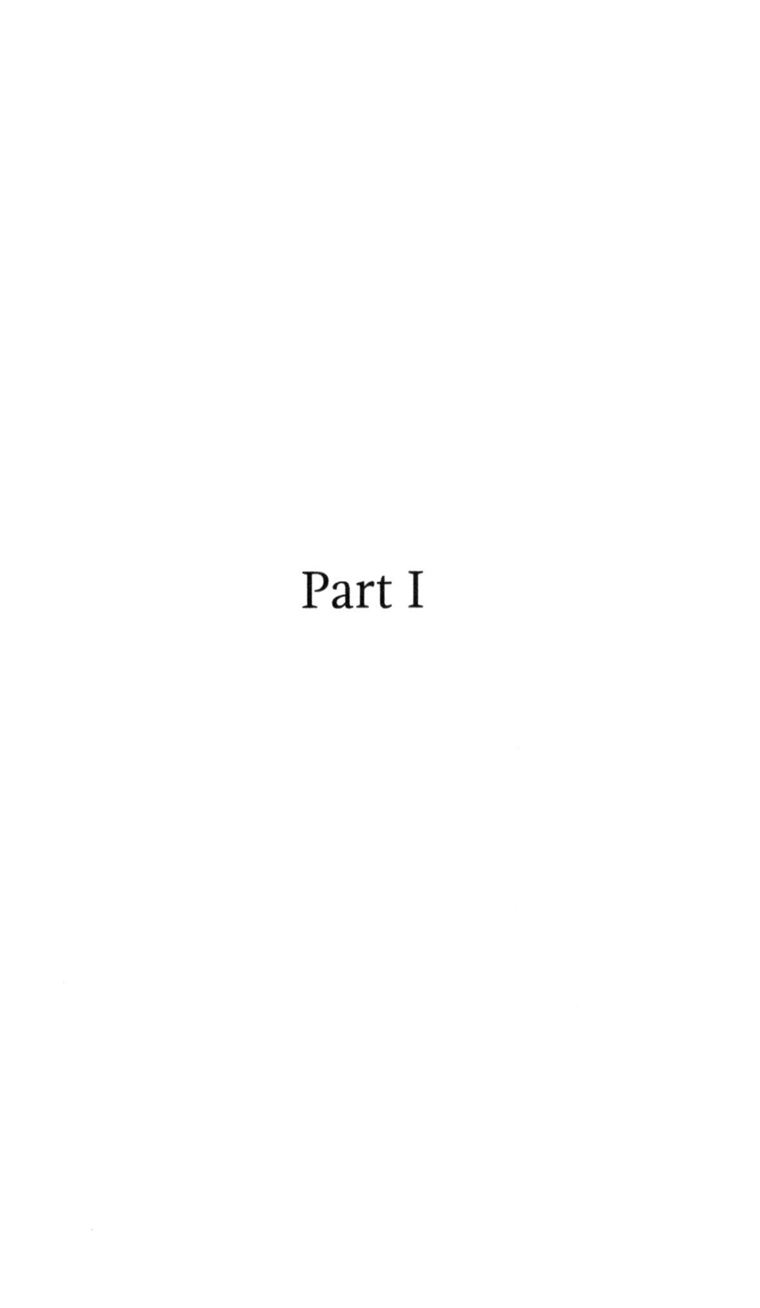

Part I

CHAPTER I

A Holistic View of Happiness

"Most folks are as happy as they make up their minds to be."
- Abraham Lincoln.

In the opening section of this book, we begin by uncovering the genuine essence of happiness and success. We delve into the idea that universal love serves as the bedrock of happiness and explore the pivotal role the mind plays in this context. We then delve into the significance of activities such as meditation, self-awareness, prayer, positive affirmations, and gratitude in elevating happiness levels. Following this, we underscore the importance of cultivating positive habits to enhance overall efficiency and productivity. To cap it all off, we provide a practical guide to daily routines that can aid you on this lifelong journey toward happiness and success.

The Significance of Happiness

Happiness has been emphasized by religions, spiritual masters, and even modern psychologists as an essential aspect of life. Spirituality teaches us to find peace in all situations, like swimming in rough seas. Research, as highlighted by Tal-Ben Shahar and Shawn Achor [1,2], has shown that happiness increases our chances of success. Learning to be happy is, therefore, the secret to achieving success.

An article in the Harvard Business Review [4] states, *"The single greatest advantage in the modern economy is a happy and engaged workforce. Happiness raises sales by 37%, productivity by 31%, and task accuracy by 19%. It also makes you more creative, popular, and healthy."*

Happiness plays a significant role in our lives. While everyone desires continuous happiness, it remains elusive for many. Happiness is not merely the presence of joy in every moment but an overall state of well-being and contentment.

As human beings, we possess the unique ability to reflect internally. We operate in both the external and inner worlds simultaneously. Our focus on external achievements often leads us to neglect our inner well-being. However, prioritizing peace and happiness can achieve external success with less effort and stress. Balancing our pursuit of external achievements with our inner happiness is crucial for overall fulfilment.

Throughout our lives, we strive to become more efficient and skilful in navigating the external world while maintaining inner peace and happiness. From a young age, we learn through experimentation and feedback mechanisms. Our experiences teach us what works and doesn't, fostering continuous growth and improvement. However, our conditioning often leads us to view these experiences as successes or failures, causing unnecessary suffering. Instead, we should strive to become the best versions of ourselves in both the external and internal realms.

Happiness is the birth right of every individual, free from any prerequisites. Helen Keller (1880-1968), a famous author and disability rights advocate, was deaf, mute, and blind and still became an inspiration to many. Nick Vujicic, born without limbs, has shown that happiness and prosperity are possible even in the face of disability. Past mistakes, failures, poverty, or ill health do not hinder our ability to find happiness. As Henry Ford famously said, *"Whether you think you can or you think you can't, you are right" also applies to happiness.*

We all cherish the company of happy individuals. A happy child, sibling, spouse, friend, colleague, or boss can uplift our mood. When we expect happiness from others, they, in turn, expect it from us.

Types of Happiness

Our innate desire for happiness can be fulfilled through various avenues. The first is sensory pleasure. In today's world, pleasure is easily accessible and can be obtained on demand. However, indulging in sensory pleasures without restraint can lead to addiction and harm.

Another form of happiness stems from achieving milestones such as academic success, job offers, wealth, possessions, recognition, and status. While these achievements bring happiness, they require intelligence, perseverance, and emotional stability. It is essential to recognize that although these milestones are desirable, they do not guarantee lasting happiness. Pursuing them relentlessly often leads to stress. However, striving to do our best, enjoying the process, and viewing these achievements as bonuses can enhance our overall well-being.

The state of "flow" provides happiness when we engage in activities, we are passionate about. It refers to being fully absorbed in a task where the difficulty level matches our skills. We experience growth when we solve problems beyond our comfort zone. One could be passionate about their job, profession, or a hobby. Some examples are music, football, programming, or product design. Whatever it may be, it is important to note that discovering our passion requires exploration, effort, and time, and therefore not everyone can find it in the profession due to real life constraints. If you do find passion in something, it will be a great stress buster.

Happiness derived from doing good for others, especially in larger groups, lasts longer than the previous forms. Providing food for the hungry during tough times or offering emotional support can bring profound happiness. However, these acts must come from natural compassion, not an obsessive need for validation. Giving brings happiness to both the giver and the receiver, strengthening bonds between individuals.

Finally, the most profound form of happiness exists without any external cause. We will explore this in detail in later chapters, focusing on practices such as meditation, prayers, gratitude, and compassion. This form of happiness is entirely within our control. Interestingly, embarking on this journey also makes it easier to achieve success in the other forms of happiness mentioned earlier.

The following stories illustrate what these forms of happiness mean in real life.

Femi Otedola, a wealthy African billionaire, shared in an interview how he experienced four stages of happiness in life before discovering its true meaning. In the first stage, he focused on accumulating wealth but found that it did not bring lasting happiness. Next, he tried collecting valuable items, realizing this failed to provide lasting happiness. In the third stage, he sought happiness through big projects, but again, it eluded him.

However, it was in the fourth stage that everything changed. A friend asked him to donate 200 wheelchairs to disabled children personally. While witnessing the joy on the faces of the children as they moved around and had fun in their new wheelchairs, he felt a profound sense of real joy inside him. As he was about to leave, one child held onto his legs and expressed the desire to remember his face so that he could recognize and thank him again in heaven. This heart-warming response made him happy and completely transformed his outlook on life.

Charles "Chuck" Feeney, nicknamed the James Bond of Philanthropy by Forbes, the 89-year cofounder of airport retailer "Duty-Free Shoppers," amassed billions of dollars living a life of monk-like frugality. As a philanthropist, he pioneered the idea of Giving While Living. Over the last four decades, he gave almost 8 billion dollars to charities, universities, and foundations. In the end, he kept very little to himself. Feeney went to great lengths to keep his donations secret. Now, he lives in an apartment in San Fransisco with an austerity of a freshman dorm room.

While we can enjoy the different types of happiness mentioned above, understanding their limitations helps us prioritize our efforts and maintain a balance. In this chapter, we will focus on happiness derived from external actions.

Our Current Situation

Just as exercise is essential for physical fitness, studying is necessary for academic success. However, if we dislike studying but desire good grades, we may achieve them through hard work, but our lives will be filled with pain and dissatisfaction. We create a cycle of continuous struggle by postponing our happiness and engaging in activities that do not bring us joy.

When Shawn Achor, a well-known author, served as a student counsellor at Harvard, he noticed that a staggering 80% of students were struggling with depression, and 10% had even thought about suicide. During this time, he also recognized his battle with depression, and his initial journal entry reflected his bleak outlook: *"I don't remember being happy, and I don't think I will ever be happy again."* Nevertheless, he transformed from a depressed high achiever into a joyful researcher dedicated to the pursuit of happiness.

Consider winning a large lottery prize. Initially, we may experience immense joy, but as time passes, worries about how to keep our money safe and manage it start consuming us. This highlights the inherent nature of our minds. No matter how good something is, we inevitably seek change after a while. Our minds crave variety and new experiences.

Furthermore, once we accomplish one goal, we immediately set our sights on a new one. The happiness derived from achieving goals is temporary. This constant pursuit of milestones leads to a relentless and often painful journey through life. Unfortunately, society often values results over the processes that lead to them.

We often dwell on past mistakes or hurts, worry about the future, and lose interest in the present moment. Ruminating on the past or constantly anticipating the future distracts us from fully experiencing and enjoying the present. It's like driving a car while continually looking in the rear-view mirror or focusing too far ahead instead of the road in front of us. Both approaches are dangerous and hinder our ability to find joy and efficiency in the present moment.

If our current approach to life does not guarantee continuous happiness, we must explore alternative ways to achieve it. Is there another path that is practical for ordinary individuals? Let us delve into how we can learn to be consistently happy.

Learning to Be Always Happy

John Milton once said, *"The mind is its own place and, in itself can make a heaven of hell or a hell of heaven."* This means that our internal state, rather than external circumstances, is responsible for our experiences. Unconsciously, we create hell even in favourable situations due to our ingrained bad habits and erroneous beliefs. Conversely, we can create heaven through conscious good habits and empowering beliefs, even in challenging circumstances.

On-demand happiness can only come from within, from things we can control all the time. Our attitude and response to people and circumstances are within our power, but we cannot control those external factors. Happiness, therefore, is an inside job—a choice—and entirely our responsibility. However, our current approach is the opposite. We expect people, circumstances, and results to change according to our desires to provide us with happiness. Unaware of our inherent power, we sit on a metaphorical throne of happiness and thus become beggars seeking happiness from external sources.

True happiness without any specific reason arises from our natural state of being. It is not something we pursue; rather, it is something we allow. Often, we struggle to be happy, unaware that our conditioned minds obscure our innate ability to experience this divine state of being. This state of being encompasses love, peace, and happiness as intertwined attributes. Unconditional, universal love leads to harmony, bringing peace of mind and happiness.Therefore, we should strive to love everything—circumstances, people, the environment, and the universe itself. In practical terms, this means accepting situations and individuals with love and making a loving effort to improve what we can. At present, we tend to dislike most things we do, considering it a natural response. However, the transition from the old mind-set of resistance to the new mind-set of acceptance cannot occur instantaneously. We must first be open to the possibility of change and then embark on a gradual learning process. This shift involves moving from a negative mind-set of resisting circumstances and people to a positive mind-set of acceptance. As we cultivate peace of mind and happiness, our thoughts and actions improve, enhancing our chances of success. The next chapter will delve deeper into this aspect. To aid us in this journey, let us consider the following prayer:

Serenity Prayer by Saint Francis: *"God! Give us strength and courage to change whatever should be changed; grace to accept with serenity the things which can't be changed; and wisdom to know the difference."*

This prayer emphasizes the importance of responding to every situation, person, or challenge to the best of our ability. We can rid ourselves of insecurity and apprehension regarding results by steering clear of negativity stemming from comparisons, competition, or win/lose scenarios. Finding satisfaction in doing our best is true happiness. As a result, we can act spontaneously and joyfully. We no longer worry about how much we can change or improve; instead, we lovingly accept and gracefully surrender the things we cannot change entirely or only partially. By relinquishing resistance, we free ourselves from anxiety, worry, and feelings of inadequacy. This peace and tranquillity allow us to be alert, wise, and efficient. Joyfulness becomes our attitude, enabling us to respond effectively to any situation. It is an ongoing attitude, not a destination.

When the weather is unfavourable, we adapt by carrying a raincoat or an umbrella. Similarly, when faced with challenges in life, we should adopt a similar approach—doing what is necessary and moving forward. Complaining about a situation only prolongs our suffering. Instead, we must do our best while protecting ourselves mentally and emotionally.

Enjoying the Process

Finding enjoyment in the journey toward our goals is crucial, not just in reaching the destination. While keeping our eyes on the peak to ensure we are heading in the right direction, we must savor the process.

The ancient Hindu spiritual text, the Bhagavad Gita, advises us to focus on our karma—what we need to do—without worrying about the outcomes of our actions. Our efforts are within our control, but the results depend on various complex factors and can never be guaranteed. If we fixate on the results, we cannot fully concentrate on the actions due to the stress and pressure. A relevant example is top-ranked football or hockey players missing a penalty kick or stroke in a crucial match, even though the probability of a save by the goalkeeper is usually low in such situations.

In the new approach, we let go of our insistence on both the fruits of our actions and the actions themselves. While we have a plan, if circumstances beyond our control prevent us from executing a particular task, we peacefully accept the situation and consider the best course of action instead of getting agitated.

Happiness in Work

Mother Teresa once said we should do every small thing with great love. This means approaching tasks with interest and attention. This idea may seem impractical initially, but we must believe it is possible, even if we don't know how to achieve it. It is a matter of practice, gradually improving our love for our work. This journey has no destination, but the process itself brings us happiness. Subsequent chapters will delve into practical ways to cultivate a love for our work, enhancing our chances of success in student life.

Our perception of the work assigned to us, rather than the work itself, determines our happiness and success. Even in routine and mundane jobs, we can find meaning and purpose. For instance, consider the perspective of three bricklayers working on a construction project. One person views the job as a means to earn a salary, while the second person sees it as a way to support their family. The third person finds happiness in the act of building a temple.

Many experts advise younger generations to focus on doing what they love to achieve success. While this advice seems sound initially, as it is evident that we excel in activities we are passionate about, it is not always easy to pursue work we love. Sometimes, our passions may not align with financially rewarding professions, and we often encounter tasks during our academic journey that we are not passionate about. Unfortunately, this dissatisfaction leads to inefficiency and diminishes our chances of success. Therefore, we must change our approach to the work we do. Saints and certain professionals possess the unique quality of approaching every task enthusiastically, but this quality can be developed through practice. In the epic Mahabharata, the main characters were skilled in wielding all weapons, even though each person was an expert in wielding a specific weapon.

Comparison and Competition

Competition arises when numerous individuals aspire to limited rewards. This applies to various fields, from education to business. However, it is crucial to determine whether competition intimidates us or if we embrace it as an enjoyable challenge. The former attitude prevents us from performing at our best and diminishes our chances of success. On the other hand, the latter approach allows us to give our best and improve our likelihood of success. Success can never be guaranteed, so what truly matters is how we participate. A failure may demotivate a negative-minded individual, but a positive person learns from the experience, enhances his skills, and increases his chances of success.

Google C.E.O. Sundar Pichai recently stated, *"I have always believed that you tend to go wrong by focusing too much on competition. Big companies, particularly, fail because they stumble internally. Your job is to focus on doing what you do better."* This principle applies to individuals as well.

Companies like Apple and Tesla succeeded by focusing on creating groundbreaking products that consumers and their competitors had never imagined before. Many Japanese automobile and consumer electronics industries have employed a similar approach. This was because they applied what Sunder Pichai said, and they always focused on doing their best and not bothering about looking over their shoulders to see what the competitors were doing.

Even in competitive environments, strategic cooperation with the right individuals benefits all parties involved. As the saying goes, *"A lone wolf dies, whereas a pack survives."* The key is to form alliances with the right people. This book provides tips and guidance to help you achieve that.

Comparison is an inherent part of human life in every field. We must accept comparison without negativity. If we approach it with the right mind-set, it can inspire us to improve. However, if envy or jealousy is involved, it creates stress. It is important to recognize that while individuals and businesses excel in certain areas, they may not excel in everything. By synergizing our efforts and collaborating, we can achieve better results together. This principle holds in academia, from undergraduate studies to Ph.D. level.

The Impact of Thinking

Negativity in any form reduces our efficiency in dealing with events and people. It leads to frustration, and we often hold others responsible for our negative experiences. This creates a vicious cycle. Understanding this detrimental cycle allows us to break free and initiate a new, positive evolution cycle. We must cease the production of complaints and start a "gratitude factory." A grateful person attracts many supporters who help him succeed in his endeavours.

If we approach exams, interviews, games, or performances with apprehension and fear of failure, our minds and brains receive negative signals, hampering our preparation and overall performance. But by remaining calm and confident, we can perform to the best of our abilities, increasing our chances of success. This principle applies to all aspects of life, including jobs, relationships, and more.

Generally, we attract circumstances and people consistent with our dominant thought patterns. Happy individuals naturally attract happiness, and vice versa.

The following real-life story illustrates the power of optimism.

Bert and John Jacobs own a multimillionaire apparel brand, "Life is Good." They and their four siblings had a challenging childhood upbringing due to poverty. Their father, dealing with severe depression and losing his hand in a car accident, expressed frustration by yelling and screaming at the children daily. Despite their struggles, their mother bravely coped with her depression, finding solace in singing, dancing, telling bedtime stories, and acting out characters from children's books. One particular dinner time ritual left a lasting impact on the brothers, helping them maintain optimism during their youth and later in their business endeavors. Their mother would ask each child to share something positive that happened during the day—a compulsory exercise that brought joy to everyone. Despite having many negative experiences in their daily lives due to poverty, they were trained to look for the silver lining in the dark clouds.

As Bert and John grew up, they ventured into selling T-shirts to college students. However, their sales were lackluster even after five years of hard work. In search of inspiration for exciting T-shirt taglines, they stumbled upon a phrase at home: "Life is Good." To their surprise, printing this optimistic message on their products led to a phenomenal increase in sales. Recognizing the secret to success—that people appreciate and respond to optimistic messages, especially in challenging times—the brothers incorporated positivity into all their products. Their venture didn't take long to skyrocket, and they soon achieved multimillionaire status.

When addressing their audiences during public speeches, Bert and John share a simple yet profound mantra: *"life is not perfect, and life is not easy. But by focusing on opportunities rather than obstacles, life is good."*

Planting Seeds for Future Harvest

It is a universal law of life that whatever seed we plant in the soil—whether good or bad—will return multiplied. Nature does not discriminate.

Typically, we expect love, respect and help from others to make us happy. This reactive approach often leads to disappointment when our expectations are not met. Instead of relying on others to make us happy, we can cultivate happiness within ourselves through practices like meditation and affirmations, loving, appreciating, and respecting ourselves first, and then extending that love to others.

Ralph Waldo Emerson once said, *"It is one of the most beautiful compensations of this life that no man can sincerely try to help another without helping himself."* Research suggests that while happier people are more likely to help others, helping others also brings happiness to the giver. Therefore, let us give to others to the extent we can, whether through prayers, appreciation, gratitude, encouragement, or any possible form of help, physical, financial, or time.

Happiness in Relationships

The renowned positive psychologists Ed Diener and Martin Seligman studied "very happy people" and found that having rich and fulfilling social relationships was the key to their happiness. Aristotle also wrote, *"Without friendship, no happiness is possible."* Building and nurturing relationships requires investment and can be achieved through the practices outlined in this book. To cultivate good relationships, we should focus on how we can contribute and give rather than solely seeking things from others. Happiness and unhappiness have a contagious effect within social circles. Surrounding ourselves with happy companions is crucial, as their happiness can positively impact us. By celebrating the success and happiness of others, we can multiply our joy.

Developing Positive Qualities

While external success and happiness are often associated with stress, we can shift our focus inward and work on developing personal qualities and skills. These qualities serve as a solid foundation for both happiness and success. They include integrity, honesty, loyalty, respect, trust, responsibility, humility, compassion, fairness, forgiveness, authenticity, courage, generosity, perseverance, kindness, optimism, reliability, conscientiousness, self-discipline, encouragement, punctuality, and thoroughness.

To improve these qualities, we can start by listing the ones we wish to enhance and then determine the order of priority. It's important to work on them one at a time, focusing on deliberate practice and self-auditing. While perfection may not be attainable, consistent effort and periodic evaluation will lead to improvement. Benjamin Franklin's autobiography [7] exemplifies how daily monitoring can support personal growth. Developing these qualities requires willpower, which can be strengthened through happiness practices.

Understanding that the motivation to cultivate positive qualities is closely tied to our mental state is crucial. When we experience happiness, developing these qualities becomes significantly easier. Happiness and these qualities work together synergistically because practicing happiness enhances and strengthens these positive traits.

Imagine if we were tasked with choosing outstanding employees or seeking meaningful relationships. The qualities we would prioritize are exactly the ones we should cultivate within ourselves. Interestingly, despite being aware of these beneficial qualities, many tend to downplay their significance, considering it fashionable not to dwell too much on them.

Understanding the Interplay of Happiness and Pain

It's crucial to recognize that what brings us happiness in one moment can bring pain in another and vice versa. Personal experiences often shape our perceptions of happiness and pain. For example, a job change that initially brought happiness may later lead to discomfort due to unforeseen circumstances. However, these situations present opportunities for growth and adaptation.

Growing up in a middle-class family, I dreamed of landing a high-paying job. So, you can imagine my delight when I was offered a position at Tata Electric Company in Mumbai after completing my Ph.D. However, my excitement was short-lived as the weather in Mumbai began to take a toll on my health, triggering severe asthma symptoms. My doctor recommended that I find a job in a different location to improve my well-being. What was once a source of happiness becoming a source of pain.

Given the challenges of finding a comparable job in a different location, I accepted an academic position at I.I.T. Delhi despite the significant pay cut. Although I knew I was passionate about research, I harboured serious doubts about my teaching ability. Feelings of apprehension and unease accompanied this career change. However, I was determined to overcome these challenges and improve my teaching skills. Throughout my student years, I have always relied on my unwavering determination and relentless work ethic to achieve my goals. During the initial teaching phase, I received honest feedback from my students, urging me to go beyond the confines of the textbook. It was a wake-up call that pushed me to delve into various books and create comprehensive teaching materials. As a result, my confidence grew, and I began to find joy in teaching. This continuous practice soon became my strong suit, shaping my entire career. Before long, I started receiving excellent feedback from my students. In fact, in the first year that the Institute began recognizing exceptional teaching, I was honored with the title "Outstanding Teacher." What initially seemed like a painful change turned out to be a profoundly fulfilling one.

Pain and Happiness Can Coexist

Although we cannot change certain events like sickness, loss of a job, or loss of a loved one, which cause pain, we have the power to act in each moment. Striving to do our best is a source of happiness regardless of the circumstances. By embracing this mind-set, we can navigate through pain while finding moments of joy and fulfillment.

The Journey of Happiness

Happiness is not an end goal but a continuous journey. Depending on our needs, we can have any goals, including wealth and fame. However, it's essential to appreciate and enjoy the process of working towards our goals. Happiness is a skill that anyone can develop. However, internal and external factors influence each person's happiness level, as we are still evolving. With practice, the base level of happiness can improve, and we can cultivate a happier mind-set.

In the upcoming chapters, we will delve into the factors that affect happiness and explore fundamental ways to enhance it. We will also discuss practical techniques and exercises to practice happiness.

• • •

CHAPTER II

Love – The Foundation of Happiness

"There is only one happiness in life, to love and be loved." - George Sand.

Love is the powerful force that binds the Universe together. Every cell in our body and mind naturally craves love. We all have an innate desire to love and be loved constantly.

Each one of us is unique yet interconnected with the world around us. Our bodies, minds, intellects, and voices are distinct from others. Our talents and aspirations also differ. We stop comparing ourselves to others when we understand and embrace this natural diversity. Loving ourselves becomes essential for inner harmony. Additionally, we share a common bond with everything in the Universe. Given our interdependence, it is vital to love the world, including current and past situations, people, other species, and the environment, to maintain harmony.

"There is more hunger for love and appreciation in this world than for bread." - Mother Teresa.

Religions were created to help humans understand life and their relationship with God or the Universe and seek assistance in resolving their problems. While religion encompasses external and internal practices, spirituality focuses solely on the internal aspects. Spirituality does not necessarily require any religious beliefs. Some religions, such as Buddhism, do not believe in the concept of God. However, universal love forms the core of all religions and spiritual practices. Thousands of years ago, the founders of religions recognized that love is the foundation of happiness. Consequently, devotional practices, common in major religions, are based on love.

Love leads to harmony, and harmony leads to peace, which is also a form of happiness. Friction arises wherever there is conflict, whether related to work we dislike or within relationships. While we are mostly aware of external conflicts, we often overlook the internal conflicts we face continuously. The frequency with which we resolve these internal conflicts plays a crucial role in our happiness and success. Love is the best tool for addressing these conflicts, acting as a lubricant in challenging situations. In Hindi, the word for "lubricant" is "Snehak," which perfectly translates to the role of love as a lubricant in our lives.

Now, let us explore why starting with ourselves is vital to happiness.

Self-Love

The most important people in our life are ourselves. We experience the world through our bodies and minds, our most essential life partners. If we are physically unwell or our minds are disturbed, even the most idyllic external circumstances will not bring us happiness.

After fulfilling our primary survival needs, self-love becomes the most critical factor in establishing the foundation for happiness and success. Just as breathing is a continuous necessity for survival, self-love must become a habit for a joyful life. Kamal Ravikant eloquently expresses this idea in his book "Love Yourself as If Your Life Depends on It" [8].

What is inside is reflected outside. When we are filled with love, we naturally radiate love and happiness in every aspect of our lives, including work. Conversely, unhappiness reflects a lack of love within us. It is not a binary situation of either having love or not. Instead, we selectively like or dislike certain parts or aspects of ourselves.

Most of our negative emotions manifest as anxiety, restlessness, irritation, jealousy, anger, and hatred, depending on the intensity of the perceived lack. Problems such as addiction, feeling overweight, ugly, short, dumb, or timid all stem from a lack of self-love.

We routinely inquire about the well-being of the people we meet, but often, it is merely a formality. Consequently, the responses we receive may not be genuine. However, when it comes to the person we love, we genuinely care about their well-being and try to understand their truth, offering support to improve their situation. Surprisingly, we don't extend the same level of inquiry to ourselves. Since we should be the ones who love ourselves the most, this self-inquiry should become a habit. We must check in with ourselves multiple times daily to assess how we are doing. If we are not doing well, we must immediately identify the exact nature of the problem to improve our situation. This will be discussed in more detail in the chapter on self-awareness.

Self-love involves engaging in self-talk, where we assure ourselves of our love. This assurance instills confidence in our ability to improve despite any imperfections. It is akin to a motherly or divine love that accepts us despite our failures, mistakes, limitations, or blunders. It does not imply that we approve of everything we do or that there is no need for improvement. On the contrary, we seek continuous growth in every area we desire. How we think, look at our bodies, touch our bodies, and talk to ourselves should all reflect deep love.

Self-love means learning to be at peace and doing our best in every simple or challenging situation. Through programming ourselves with self-love, our minds gradually accept this notion, even if we initially have doubts. Over time, our beliefs, values, and character become refined. The harmony between our desires, thoughts, and actions improves naturally. This, in turn, enhances our work efficiency, health, relationships, and creativity without us explicitly striving for them. It's like a miracle cure. These aspects establish a solid foundation for increased happiness and success. Developing kindness and compassion for ourselves is more important than others.

Self-Love Affirmation Exercise: Mirror Exercise

Stand in front of a mirror, focusing on your own eyes. Smile and say with genuine feeling, "(Your Name), I love you and accept you as you are." Ideally, repeat this affirmation 15 times. If time is limited, you can repeat it once or twice. Practice this exercise at least twice daily, preferably in the morning and before bed. You can also incorporate similar affirmations whenever you visit the washroom [8,9].

Most of us will initially struggle to believe these words when we say them. However, we must continue the practice despite our initial doubts. It is an ongoing exercise, not a short-term solution. As we repeat the affirmation, our belief in it grows unconsciously. It is crucial to remember that self-love is a lifelong journey.

Kamal Ravikant, an author, and entrepreneur, shares his experience of transforming his life from financial, health, and relationship challenges to a dramatically improved state by consistently practicing self-love affirmations throughout the day for several months [8].

Louise Hay, the author of several books, including the renowned "Heal Your Life" [9], describes how we can transform our lives through self-love. Her inspiring story details how she changed her life from despair, depression, and cancer through self-love, forgiveness, and naturopathy.

My wife, who is short and overweight, was overwhelmed by her research, teaching, and other activities as an I.I.T. professor. She hardly had any time to think about anything else. Despite this, she would often feel resentful and dislike her physical appearance, imagining herself as a slim and tall person in her next life. After wasting many precious years, she realized she was never relaxed, content, or happy. After my persistent suggestions, she began practicing self-love. Upon waking up, she would visualize hugging herself and appreciating each part of her body and organs with great love and gratitude, acknowledging how amazingly they cooperated even in challenging situations. Gradually, she became calmer and calmer; today, she hardly gives any importance to her physical appearance.

Walking Mantra

We can also incorporate self-love affirmations as a walking mantra. Whenever we have a moment, we can silently repeat a self-love affirmation. It is such an easy practice that we can do it anytime, anywhere. We can even utilize the hourly chime on our watches or phones to remind us to do a self-love affirmation. We often find ourselves waiting in various daily situations without any specific task. These moments provide an opportunity to do a few self-love affirmations. We can also make it a habit to begin significant events or activities with a self-love affirmation. No one else will ever notice, but it instantly makes us feel good.

We can start by incorporating self-love affirmations into our daily to-do list. Doing just one affirmation is so simple that there is no excuse not to begin. Once we experience the positive impact, we will feel motivated to do more. Soon, the momentum will build up, and we may find ourselves naturally doing multiple affirmations throughout the day. It is the best addiction and is the master key to joyful living.

Self-Esteem

We are all imperfect in various ways. Our duty in life is to accept ourselves lovingly with our weaknesses without judgment. This unconditional and steadfast support for ourselves, despite our limitations, challenging circumstances, and setbacks, is crucial for enhancing self-esteem.

Developing a habit of noticing and acknowledging our good deeds creates a virtuous cycle. It motivates us to do more and builds self-esteem. Before going to bed, we can take a moment to appreciate the good things we have done during the day. These accomplishments can range from significant achievements to acts of discipline and even avoiding temptations. It's important to remember that these need not be grand gestures; anything that makes us feel good about ourselves is worth acknowledging.

Self-esteem is supposed to be an internal assessment. However, we often rely on others' judgments to determine our self-worth. No matter how hard we try, we can never always please everyone. This futile exercise only leads to stress and sets us up for a lifetime of unhappiness. Our thinking, beliefs, practices, and behaviors greatly impact our self-esteem. We must have confidence in our ability to face challenges and cultivate a sense of control over our lives to maintain good self-esteem. We must firmly believe that we have the right to happiness and deserve happiness. Nathaniel Branden [10] suggests six practices to improve self-esteem:

1. Living Consciously: Being aware of our choices, reasons, and the consequences they bring.

2. Self-Acceptance: Valuing and respecting ourselves, including our emotional experiences.
3. Self-Responsibility: Accepting responsibility for our desires, choices, actions, behaviour, communication, and overall happiness.
4. Self-Assertiveness: Honouring our wants, needs, and values and expressing them appropriately. We must also learn to stand up for ourselves.
5. Living Purposefully: Setting reasonable goals and creating action plans to achieve them.
6. Personal Integrity: When our ideals, convictions, standards, beliefs, and behavior are aligned, we have integrity.

By incorporating these practices into our lives, we can improve our self-esteem and cultivate a healthier relationship with ourselves.

Incorporating love, particularly self-love, into our lives is a transformative practice that can bring significant positive changes. We lay a solid foundation for happiness and success by embracing self-love and nurturing a deep appreciation and acceptance of ourselves. It is a lifelong journey that requires consistent effort and practice. As we explore the various aspects of love and its role in our lives, we will discover more strategies and practices to enhance our overall well-being and empower us to lead a fulfilling and successful life.

Love Your Body

Our body is the only vehicle we have in this life. What we do right now determines how it will perform decades later. There is no point in comparing it with others. We must express gratitude daily for what we have and take the best care to ensure the best possible performance.

Touching our body with a lot of love and gratitude or visualizing a tight hug with tons of thanks for being with us and cooperating is quite soothing. Let us express love and gratitude to it as many times a day as possible. We can do it while taking a bath as well. We can do it at least twice, once in the morning and before bed.

The body needs a balanced diet to keep it healthy and energetic. It also needs adequate rest and sleep to recharge. Moreover, it needs sufficient exercise to keep it strong and healthy. At least five days a week, a minimum of thirty minutes of brisk walking is essential. However, those who can do jogging or other vigorous exercises can do it instead. Exercise is a great stress buster. A strong and healthy body improves work efficiency, reduces sick days, makes you happy and confident, and enhances your personality.

Exercise Benefits Body and Mind: In a study on exercise benefits for depressed people [6], 1st group was put on antidepressants, 2nd group was told to exercise 45 minutes per day three times a week, and the 3rd group was asked to do both. When examined four months later, all groups had similar improvements. The relapse rate after six months was 38 % for the 1st group, 31 % for the 3rd, and only 9 % for the 2nd.

Exercise is an incredibly powerful mood lifter, and the effects last longer. We can walk, bike, run, play, stretch, jump, or rope.

Sleep Better

Fatigue heavily impairs our ability to remain positive. Hence, about eight hours of peaceful sleep is essential. Students rarely understand the critical importance of sleep and rest. In this period, the body and mind recharge for efficient functioning the next day. Although life in the last century has changed fast, the human biology energy recharge mechanism has remained virtually unchanged. Seventy-five percent of high growth hormones (HGH) are released in sleep; the maximum burst is between 10-12 P.M. The best duration for rest is between 10 P.M. to 6 A.M.

Most students generally tend to sleep quite late and wake up late. However, it is quite harmful. In addition to the ineffective body and mind recharge, it makes the morning stressful. Right from brushing teeth, bath, and breakfast, everything is rushed. The bed and room are also disorganized. It is important to note that you carry this mood throughout the day. Doing the opposite to start the day feeling peaceful and energetic would be best. Early waking up makes it possible.

It may not be possible to change this lifestyle suddenly. Hence, it is better to experiment and check the benefits by practicing stepwise. First, set the alarm for sleep commencement and wake up at your comfort level for a week. That means absolutely no change in sleep hours. However, you will notice that regularity makes you feel better. Do not change the timings unless there is an emergency. Next week, if you sleep and wake up late, advance both alarms by just ten minutes. The mind will not resist such a small change. Check how you feel. If you feel good, you may try further advancement by ten minutes. You can stop this experiment as soon as you feel uncomfortable. If your number of sleep hours is more than eight, the next experiment is to try and reduce it by ten minutes every week until you reach the desired one. You can advance just the waking up time for this. Again, do not continue this experiment if you don't feel better.

A short fifteen-minute nap after lunch reduces stress and provides quick body recharge. We can take three deep, mindful breaths whenever we feel stressed or lack energy.

We will immediately feel better.

Love Others

When we interact with others, some friction is inevitable because of the differences in temperaments and perceptions. No one is good or bad, right or wrong; we are different. However, love acts as lubrication to make relationships mutually beneficial. Because of our expectations from others, we generally love them conditionally. Relationships that have a lot of possessiveness and mistrust will harm love. Love doesn't have to be exclusive to a few; we can love many persons. Love is consideration, caring, and sharing with others. It also requires reverence for others. Love binds people, and fear separates them. Every person has both good and bad qualities inside them. Finding faults with others comes naturally to us. But we should focus on finding good as well in others. What we deliberately look for in others and within us grows in us. For harmony outside, loving other human beings is essential. For this, we need to cooperate and empower each other. Appreciation and gratitude for the help we receive are the most important things. Let us rejoice in the good acts of others as well.

We (myself and my wife) have significantly benefitted from the following practice. Whenever we observed friction brewing with someone, we made it a point to pray for their welfare and communicate with them by visualizing in thoughts, appreciating their good qualities, showing concern for their ongoing struggles, and wishing them blessings from God. We found a distinct reduction of disharmony in almost all cases.

We must not cause intentional harm to others through our actions or words. We may do good things for others or express good words to avoid conflict or impress others most of the time. However, we may continue to harbor negative thoughts toward others. We feel that our thoughts don't harm anyone because no one knows what we think. Understanding that thoughts are also karma and have consequences like words and actions is essential. Moreover actions and words are far fewer than thoughts. The consequences of all these things determine our fate. Thoughts have maximum effect in this. Harmony in thoughts, words, and actions is essential for happiness.

We can help others in need in diverse ways, physically, financially, or psychologically. Let us do whatever is feasible, considering our strengths and limitations. Praying for the welfare of others doesn't cost anything and can be done anytime. Hence, this is the minimum thing to do. Loving others means creating a vast army of well-wishers who help us in many ways. Increased happiness and productivity are then bound to happen.

Having good relationships with family, friends, and colleagues is the greatest asset in times of challenge. It makes us feel energetic, happier, productive, and resilient. We can greet known persons with a smile and say a warm "Hello," looking into their eyes. We can also perform a few conscious acts of kindness every day. One of the longest research studies at Harvard, over 70 years, has shown that happy social relationships are common in happy and successful persons [1].

If we want good friends, we need to become the one first. Patient and mindful listening to others show love and respect, which improves bonds. Let us greet our friends with warmth and a smile whenever we meet them. We can compliment others about every small, good thing they do and express sincere gratitude for any little help they render to us. Let us help any friend down for any reason to the extent possible. Let us pray, hug, or pat his/her back if nothing else is possible. These actions promote empathy and rapport. Helping others is a good buffer against depression.

Maintaining minimum interaction with hostile persons who waste our time, spoil our mood, and disempower us is essential. We should seek out and spend more time with happy people. We need to deepen the relationships through love and caring. We can share our goals, joys, and sorrows with them. "Good Company" is essential for progress and is one of worldly life's simplest and most essential happiness interventions. They will lift our mood when we are down, motivate us to do the right things when we feel demotivated, and take care of us if we are unwell.

At a young age, the need for a relationship is natural. However, it is essential not to get obsessed or desperate. Such an approach has harmed many careers. The best way to attract a partner is to become the right one. The happiness practice precisely achieves this objective. I have seen quite a few instances of a handsome and successful boy marrying an ordinary-looking girl and a beautiful, higher-qualified girl marrying an ordinary-looking and less successful person because of the other person's inner beauty. These people understood lifelong happiness is far more important than short-lived external beauty.

Loving others doesn't mean allowing others to exploit or harm us. We need to use our discretion in dealing with those who are inimical to us. We must understand that our love for others does not necessarily mean reciprocating the same. What love allows us to do is to take whatever necessary actions in dealing with such persons peacefully. Only then will our efforts be most effective.

Love Your Work

We need to do work in both professional and personal lives. Most of us do our professional work because of fear of losing out to others or the allure of the rewards of good work. Since both are comparison and competition-based, stress and unhappiness generation are automatic. Unlike in professional work, there is no apparent reward for doing work in personal life. Hence, most chores appear mundane, and we tend to resist and dislike them. We do it reluctantly. The result is again stress and unhappiness. However, as explained in the previous chapter, as Mother Teresa and Serenity Prayer advocates, if we practice doing whatever needs to be done in all spheres of life with love and accepting situations and persons without resistance, we can be happier and successful.

Love Nature and the Universe

We are just a tiny part of this vast Universe that sustains us. It provides air, water, food, and other essential survival resources. Gratitude and prayers are necessary for their tremendous contribution to our lives. We must also do what we can to improve the environment. We must pay this small rent to utilize the immense services of the Universe. We can take a short walk in a green area to de-stress ourselves. Walking barefoot on the grass is very good. Talking to nature brings peace.

Whenever I walk outside, I like to touch the leaves and trunks of trees and express love.

Love, Happiness, and Good Qualities

As we improve our self-love and happiness, our thinking, words, and actions improve, and we have less need for negative emotions like fear, anger, jealousy, and envy. In the light of this, we gradually become more truthful, disciplined, trustworthy, punctual, empathetic, courageous, and hardworking. There are many other qualities mentioned in the first chapter which also improve. More importantly, these gradual improvements happen without explicitly working on them. We know how vital these things are for our success in the external world. There are many tips available for avoiding procrastination. However, these will never work unless we have some degree of positivity. It is like building mental strength.

In the next chapter, we will see how the mind's role is critical in happiness.

• • •

CHAPTER III

Harnessing the Power of Our Mind

"The measure of success is happiness and peace of mind." - Bobby Davro

In our journey toward success, it is essential to understand the workings of our minds. Most of us only utilize a small fraction of our minds and brains because we lack a comprehensive understanding of their importance and functionality. Unfortunately, no formal education teaches us how to tap into the full potential of our minds. This chapter aims to provide valuable insights, making it easier for you to relate and comprehend.

Conscious and Subconscious Minds

Two distinct compartments exist within our minds: the subconscious and the conscious. The subconscious mind is the larger of the two, serving as a vast storehouse of memories, like a computer hard disk. On the other hand, the conscious mind is smaller and operates through beliefs, values, intellect, and working memory. The conscious mind has limited memory capacity, and to prevent its overloading, nonessential things are pushed to the subconscious mind. Astonishingly, brain research reveals that the subconscious mind's database is ten million times larger than the conscious mind's.

Our conscious mind interacts with the external world through our senses, but the information it collects is not flawless due to the limitations of our sensory perception. The data is then processed through the filters of our values and beliefs, which are also imperfect. Consequently, the impressions stored in the subconscious may not always be accurate.

During the Stone Age, when survival threats were prevalent, a part of our brain developed to scan for potential dangers. Although physical threats have significantly diminished over time, the brain continues to play the same role. Instead of merely perceiving physical threats, it now perceives psychological pain as a threat. This perception has given rise to a phantom in our minds called the ego. The ego constantly compares and feels insecure, regardless of whether one is an achiever or a non-achiever. Recognizing the ego as the primary cause of unhappiness, various religions and spiritual practices have emphasized the need to overcome it. Insecurity leads to greed, selfishness, and jealousy.

We continuously sow seeds of thought in our subconscious minds [11]. We are often unaware that the harmful seeds result from habitual thinking. As we sow in our subconscious mind, so shall we reap in our body and conscious mind. Consider our subconscious mind a fertile soil bed where good and bad seeds can sprout and flourish. The conscious mind acts as the navigator of our mental ship. It is aware of the objective world and acquires knowledge through observation, experience, and education. Its most significant function is reasoning using intellect. The subconscious mind follows the orders given by the conscious mind without questioning them.

Our subconscious mind perceives intuitively. It is the seat of emotions and the repository of memory. It operates at its highest capacity when our conscious mind is inactive, such as during sleep or in a drowsy state. The subconscious mind never rests, and it houses our wisdom. Wise individuals regularly consult their subconscious minds.

For achieving health, happiness, and peace, it is crucial to understand the roles of these two minds and utilize them harmoniously. The mind is an extraordinary instrument if used correctly [12]. However, if misused, it can be highly destructive. We are all aware of the challenges of controlling our minds, as our conscious mind is almost always active, except during deep sleep.

Reducing Unnecessary Mind Chatter

Most of us engage in a continuous internal dialogue within our minds if we pay attention [13]. As mentioned earlier, our ego creates insecurities in every situation, masquerading as our best friend and advisor. We may notice that this mind chatter increases during fear and stress. Even without stress, the mind indulges in self-talk, attempting to interpret the outside world and provide a sense of control, even though we cannot control external circumstances. The ego convinces us that it is our protector. Whether this dialogue is positive or negative, it prevents us from focusing on our tasks, which is detrimental. Once we understand this, we can internally signal that we no longer require this protection.

The mind has taken on the responsibility of making life okay for us. It desires universal approval and favorable situations, which is impossible to achieve. As a result, we experience numerous worries, anxiety, stress, and fear. When we accept life as it is, we can wake up in the morning, eagerly look forward to our tasks, and give our best effort. This mind-set makes work, relationships, exercise, and relaxation enjoyable.

The most effective way to reduce this mind chatter is to become aware of it. We can view ourselves as observers or security guards, simply noticing the chatter without attempting to stop it. We should avoid getting entangled in the stories, whether positive or negative, worldly or spiritual. When thieves know they are being watched, they retreat. The watchman takes no specific action but achieves the desired result [12]. By gently disengaging from this chatter, we deny it the energy it needs to persist. Gradually, the habit of self-talk diminishes, allowing us to conserve our time and energy, resulting in improved task performance.

Emotion: The Body's Reaction to Our Mind

Emotion reflects our mind in the body, which can be positive or negative [12]. For instance, an attack or negative thought generates an accumulation of energy in the body, which we identify as anger. The body prepares itself for a fight. The feeling of physical or psychological threat leads to body contraction, which we recognize as fear. Since thoughts come and go rapidly, it is challenging to monitor them. However, emotions, being a slow-motion replay in the body, are more accessible to observe. Emotions faithfully mirror our thoughts, not only during actual events but also during recollection. They provide essential feedback for enhancing our lives, and we will explore how to utilize them effectively in the Emotional Intelligence section.

Positive emotions flood the brain with dopamine and serotonin, commonly known as the feel-good chemicals, while activating the brain's learning centres at a higher level. This facilitates the organization of new information, enhances information retention, and accelerates information retrieval. Positive emotions also enable the brain to create and switch neural connections more effectively, resulting in quicker and more creative thinking. Additionally, they enhance our problem-solving and analytical skills and open our minds to innovative approaches [2].

Pain and happiness are integral aspects of our existence, serving as feedback mechanisms to inform us about the state of things. Both carry valuable messages, and receiving the message while allowing the messenger to pass through is essential. Physical pain is a warning sign indicating potential harm from ailments or external factors. Emotional pain and happiness, on the other hand, are products of our beliefs and mind-set. Our natural inclination is to avoid pain, but suppressing emotions can lead to suffering and even contribute to physical ailments. Therefore, it is crucial to learn how to observe the flow of emotional energy through our bodies without resisting or feeling overwhelmed. Developing emotional intelligence involves recognizing the correlation between our beliefs and the emotions we experience.

Within our vast storehouse of memories, each memory carries a detailed description of an event and is accompanied by associated energy. Our attachment or aversion to these experiences and the intensity of the emotions involved can lead to energy blockages, trapping the energy. A specific memory resurfaces when triggered, allowing us to observe and let it go instead of suppressing it. Both processes involve pain, but the former allows us to release it permanently. Although it may cause momentary discomfort, it is preferable compared to attempting to manipulate people and circumstances to avoid repeatedly getting hurt. Such avoidance is impossible and only results in ongoing pain and energy wastage. It is akin to keeping a thorn in your foot and avoiding contact with it. Removing the thorn with a sharp object may cause temporary pain, but it is a simpler and more effective solution.

Operating System of the Mind

Within our minds, we possess an operating system based

on the functioning of our brain and mind. This operating system consists of our beliefs and values, which shape our thoughts, actions, and overall world perception.

Beliefs

Beliefs are formed based on our interpretation of events and experiences. Whenever we encounter a situation, our mind quickly labels it as either a pain or pleasure experience, depending on our conditioning. It then accesses our subconscious memory to find similar instances from the past, leading to the formation of beliefs. The frequency and intensity of these experiences strengthen our beliefs, even though they may not always be accurate or objectively true. It's important to note that our family, society, religion, and the media can influence our beliefs. These beliefs are biased interpretations and can limit our capabilities, creating a fear-driven mind-set and negative beliefs. However, by questioning the correctness of our beliefs, we can reinterpret our experiences and create new empowering beliefs.

Shawn Achor, the famous author, said, *"If you could change someone's belief about the world, it dramatically changes their outcomes- business outcomes, their education outcomes, their health outcomes."*

For example, having positive beliefs such as "There are enough opportunities for those who keep exploring" or "Through sincere efforts, I can improve myself" can enhance our potential and lead to greater success. Conversely, negative beliefs such as "Why does this always happen to me?" or "I am not good enough" can hold us back from reaching our goals. It's crucial to recognize that beliefs are not fixed and can be changed if we consciously challenge and reshape them.

The Power of Belief

While domesticating an elephant, a baby elephant is tied to a pole with a rope. Initially, it struggles to break free but eventually learns it cannot. As the elephant grows, it becomes physically powerful enough to uproot trees. However, due to its early conditioning, it believes it cannot break free, even when restrained by a simple rope. Our minds operate similarly, clinging to outdated beliefs unless we actively challenge them.

The Harvard Study of Belief in a Math Test demonstrated the impact of comments on performance. Asian women were given positive and negative suggestions before taking a math test. When told that women are bad at math, their test performance suffered. However, when informed that Asians excel in math, their performance significantly improved. This experiment underscores the importance of positive belief and how it can influence our abilities and outcomes in all aspects of life. When we understand how suggestions by others can affect us, we can use them to our advantage through deliberate, positive self-talk, which will be discussed later.

Arunima Sinha, a basketball player from Uttar Pradesh, faced a traumatic incident when she was thrown off a running train while defending herself against a group of goons. Her leg was severely injured and required multiple fractures to heal. During her recovery in a Delhi hospital, she made a remarkable decision—to climb Mt. Everest and show the world what physically disabled individuals are capable of. With a prosthetic leg and a rod in her other leg, she conquered all seven of the world's highest peaks. Arunima believes that the true disability that holds us back is not physical but mental.

Similarly, we often find ourselves limited by negative past

experiences, failing to seize new opportunities for growth and improvement. It is not a lack of skills or aptitude that hinders us, but rather a lack of belief in our capabilities. We must recognize the conditioning and question our learned helplessness, paving the way for a mind-set primed for success.

Learned Pessimist Versus Learned Optimist

Beliefs can either limit or empower us. Dr. Seligman introduced the 3P model of a "Learned Pessimist," which illustrates disempowering beliefs: personal ("Why does this happen to only me?"), pervasive ("Why does it happen to everything I do?"), and permanent ("Why does this thing always happen to me?"). To counteract these negative beliefs, we can become "Learned Optimists" by finding specific and temporary causes for our challenges. By consciously questioning the correctness of our beliefs and reinterpreting our experiences, we can cultivate empowering beliefs that fuel our growth and success.

Embracing Life's Challenges

Life presents various challenges that can leave us physically, economically, or emotionally injured. We may experience intense pain, fall, or feel utterly exhausted. However, after tending to our wounds with love and giving ourselves adequate rest, we must choose to rise again and do our best in any given situation. Every experience, action, or behaviour of others can teach us valuable lessons for our evolution.

Growth Versus Fixed Mind-set

We will explore the concept of mind-set and its profound impact on our ability to achieve expertise and success. We will delve into the differences between a fixed mind-set and a growth mind-set, examining how our beliefs about our abilities can shape our experiences and outcomes. Let us begin by understanding the fundamental distinctions between these mind-sets.

Fixed Mind-set: The Limiting Belief

Some individuals hold a fixed mind-set, which assumes that abilities and qualities are fixed and unchangeable. They often feel the need to constantly prove themselves and may experience stress and self-doubt. However, history has shown us that many individuals who are initially considered ordinary or faced rejection achieved great success through a strong growth mind-set. Famous figures like Tolstoy, Darwin, Edison, and countless actors defied their critics and surpassed expectations through their belief in growth and development.

Growth Mind-set: Embracing Challenges and Success

In contrast, a growth mind-set fosters a love for challenges, a belief in the power of effort, a passion for learning, and resilience in the face of setbacks. Those with a growth mind-set understand that intelligence and abilities can be developed through dedication and hard work. They view challenges as opportunities for growth and embrace them with enthusiasm. Infants naturally exemplify this growth mind-set as they fearlessly persevere in acquiring new skills like walking and talking, undeterred by mistakes or failures.

The Language of Mind-set

The way we describe our failures and setbacks can reveal our mind-set. When we say, "I failed," we acknowledge a specific failed action or outcome. However, when we declare, "I am a failure," we adopt a fixed mind-set, attaching a permanent label to our entire being. It is crucial to be mindful of our language and recognize that failures do not define us.

Cultivating a Growth Mind-set

It is possible to have a fixed mind-set in certain areas of

our lives while embracing a growth mind-set in others. However, awareness of both mind-sets is essential for personal growth. Without awareness, we may inadvertently slip from a growth mind-set to a fixed one when faced with failures or challenges. By consciously cultivating a growth mind-set, we can develop the belief that effort and perseverance can make us smarter, more intelligent, and more successful.

Embracing Challenges for Growth

We have witnessed that facing challenging problems strengthens us physically, mentally, and intellectually. Conversely, we limit our growth potential by constantly seeking an easy life, avoiding difficulties, and opting for comfort.

Abundance vs. Scarcity Mind-set

When we have a scarcity mind-set, we often perceive ourselves as victims [14]. This mind-set can leave us feeling stressed, tense, low on energy, frustrated, overwhelmed, powerless, confused, and disorganized. We become fixated on what's not working and fail to see the possibilities around us. However, embracing an abundance mind-set makes us feel more relaxed and alert. We become aware of the numerous options, choices, and resources available. Our brains are designed to focus on what we believe or look for. By intentionally directing our attention and energy towards noticing the abundance around us, we open new doors, and it seems the universe is working in our favor. The truth is the universe is abundant, and we must learn how to tap into this abundance. Here are examples of statements that reflect a scarcity mind-set: "There are limited opportunities." "I don't have time." "Good people are rare."

In contrast, an abundance mind-set is reflected in

statements like: "There are ample opportunities for those who make an effort." "Goodness exists in everyone if we know how to bring it out." "I have enough time to do what I can."

"Have to" versus. "Want to" Mind-set

The way we approach our tasks and responsibilities in life can be categorized into two mind-sets: the "have to" mind-set and the "want to" or "choose to" mind-set [1]. The difference between these two mind-sets significantly impacts our happiness and work efficiency.

When we approach something with a "have to" mind-set, it implies compulsion. Our minds resist this compulsion, leading to unhappiness and decreased work efficiency. On the other hand, the "want to" or "choose to" mind-set indicates a deliberate choice. It brings enthusiasm and a sense of ownership, leading to greater happiness and improved work efficiency. We must be clear about how we approach our work.

In the words of Viktor Frankl [6], *"Everything can be taken away from a man but one thing: the last of human freedoms-to choose one's attitude in any given set of circumstances."*

Values

Values are the guiding principles that shape our life decisions, actions, and priorities. They are what we consider valuable and are like the GPS that navigates our journey. However, many of us don't give much thought to our values and allow external influences, such as media, social networks, and societal norms, to shape them. These external sources often present unrealistic images of success and happiness, leading to a misalignment between our true values and aspirations.

Values can be permanent or temporary. The external achievement-related values are temporary, whereas those related to our inner being are permanent. The values must be in harmony with our spirit; otherwise, conflict and pain exist. The values also have a hierarchy. The wrong order of priorities in values also creates pain. Hence, like beliefs, we must also become aware of our values, priority order, and harmony with our inner self. If values do not make us happy, we must replace them or change priorities.

Characteristics of Empowering and Disempowering Values

Empowering Values are [5,15] 1. Reality-based, 2. Socially constructive, and 3. Immediate and controllable.

Disempowering values are superstitious, socially destructive, and not immediate or not controllable.

Honesty is a good value because we can control it; it reflects reality and benefits others. On the other hand, popularity is a value that is out of our control. It isn't based on fact because you don't know what others think about you. Some examples of good, healthy values are standing up for oneself and others, self-respect, charity, humility, etc.

Luck

According to Psychology Professor Richard Wiseman, our perception of luck is shaped by our attitude. He suggests that luck favors those who embrace opportunities. An interesting phenomenon occurs when we desperately need to find a parking spot but can't seem to find one. This happens because our anxiety narrows our focus, causing us to overlook vacant spots that someone who is not anxious would notice. This principle applies to various aspects of life.

Even in the U.S.A.'s worst economic recession of the 1930s, some individuals and organizations were successful because they focused on spotting opportunities.

Many Grand Slam Tennis matches have witnessed players

making astonishing comebacks after being just one point away from defeat. Some people attribute these wins to pure luck. Still, they result from the players' determination and ability to focus on one ball at a time rather than being fixated on the outcome.

While being surrounded by good and helpful people is often considered lucky, we must remember that developing this skill is within the reach of anyone. Genuine love and compassion for others, expressed through words and actions, can cultivate strong connections and support from those around us.

Nature of Our Thoughts [16]

We typically associate our words and actions with karma, which shapes our future through cause and effect. However, we overlook that our thoughts also play a significant role in creating our karma. Even if we refrain from speaking ill of others or causing harm, nurturing negative thoughts about them generates a negative karmic effect. Since our thoughts outnumber our words and actions, avoiding negativity towards anyone becomes crucial.

Experts classify thoughts into four categories: pure (positive and selfless), necessary (neutral regarding actions and duties), negative (resentment, hatred, anger), and wasteful (focused on the past or future). Surprisingly, the last two categories comprise approximately 95% of our thoughts, resulting in an enormous waste of time and energy.

Attempting to eliminate negative thoughts forcefully is ineffective. Instead, it's how we handle them that truly matters. Just as an unwelcome guest will not visit again if ignored, negative thoughts can be diminished by consciously diverting our attention away from them. True freedom lies in letting go of thoughts that do not serve us.

Our minds tend to retain negative experiences more vividly than positive ones. Research indicates that it takes nearly three positive experiences to counteract the impact of a single negative experience.

Thoughts always precede any manifestation in the external world. Our subconscious mind cannot distinguish between reality and imagination. Consequently, we must deliberately program our minds with positive and uplifting thoughts, even if the current circumstances may not be ideal.

When we consistently and passionately focus on specific thoughts, our subconscious mind becomes programmed accordingly, driving us to act and accelerate the manifestation process.

We must focus on what we desire rather than what we wish to avoid. Whatever we concentrate on tends to grow and materialize in our lives. For instance, instead of saying, "I don't want to fail," we should affirm, "I love to succeed," when striving for success. Similarly, when aiming to be punctual, we should affirm, "I love to be punctual," rather than thinking, "I don't want to be late." By doing so, we increase the likelihood of achieving our desired outcome.

To change our results, we must adopt different thinking patterns and behaviours. We often overlook that our thinking tends to be conditioned and repetitive. Hence, changing our beliefs becomes crucial in transforming our thinking. This can be accomplished by exposing our minds to fresh material, such as reading new self-help or spiritual books or seeking guidance from mentors or trusted friends. When we experience hurt or loss, it is not our fault. However, repeatedly dwelling on these experiences intensifies the pain and strengthens the neural pathways associated with them. We are responsible for perpetuating this cycle of misery, not those who initially caused the harm. The solution lies in taking prudent and necessary actions in response to the hurt or loss and accepting it as a valuable lesson. It is essential to move forward without incessantly revisiting the memories.

By labelling negative thoughts as negative or wasteful, we diminish their power over us. Similarly, we can label our negative emotions as unhappy, angry, fearful, or mixed, gaining control over them. Failures should be seen as opportunities for growth, and consciously focusing on even the smallest positive aspects can elevate our mood.

We know the need to keep our bodies clean and germ-free through regular bathing and handwashing. However, we often overlook that our minds can become contaminated by worries, stress, anxiety, and negative emotions, leading to significant health issues. Understanding this allows us to employ simple techniques to cleanse our minds and improve our well-being, job performance, relationships, and happiness.

Like the body requires rest, nourishment, and exercise to maintain good health, the mind also necessitates care. While many know how to keep the body healthy, only a few know how to do the same for the mind. Engaging in meditation disciplines the mind and provides much-needed rest. It is important to remember that negative and positive thoughts consume our mental energy, although the latter is beneficial to a certain extent. Practices of prayer, affirmations, expressing gratitude, and reading uplifting material nourish the mind. These activities can be incorporated multiple times throughout the day, and it is beneficial to have a collection of materials that improve our mood and boost our confidence.

Facing Fear

Fear is a natural response designed to protect us from danger. However, in today's world, physical threats are rare, and our brain perceives psychological threats as potential dangers, causing mental anguish. Everyone experiences fear, but how we respond to it is crucial. Often, it is not failure that we fear but rather the fear of punishment or humiliation that accompanies it. These fears can become deeply ingrained during childhood and continue to harm us as adults. To overcome irrational fears that hold us back, we must examine them logically, take small steps forward while remaining vigilant, and learn from our experiences. When confronting our fears head-on, we often discover that they are not as threatening as we once believed. As Norman Vincent Peale wisely said, *"Do the things you fear, and the death of fear is certain."* Susan Jeffers captured this sentiment perfectly in her book "Feel the Fear and Do it Anyway."

Writing down our fears and their reasons creates a psychological distance and reduces their power over us. Additionally, assigning a numerical rating to the level of fear on a scale of 1-10 helps us gain perspective. When excessive fear arises, we can employ a breath control technique to interrupt its hold on us. By inhaling to a count of four, holding our breath for a count of four, and exhaling to a count of four, we can repeat this process until we feel a sense of calmness [17].

Uncertainty

Uncertainty is an inherent aspect of life. However, our brains perceive anything unknown as a potential threat. Since ancient times, our brains have been wired to respond with a "fight or flight" mechanism when faced with uncertainties. We can draw a parallel between driving at night and driving during the day to understand how to approach uncertainty. When driving at night, our visibility is limited to the distance illuminated by our vehicle's headlights. We can safely navigate hundreds of kilometres by focusing on the immediate vicinity. Similarly, we must concentrate on the present moment's needs and give our best effort. By remaining clear and present, we can alleviate stress and find happiness.

Uncertainty and constant change can be viewed as exciting or frightening, depending on our perspective. If we embrace uncertainty as an opportunity for growth, we will eagerly anticipate new experiences. Growth often occurs when we step outside our comfort zones.

Worries

Both competent and incompetent individuals worry about the future because we fear it may not meet our expectations or worsen. This worry stems from our inability to navigate an uncertain future. Hardworking and lazy people experience worry, making it seem like a natural and inevitable response. However, worrying is an unproductive habit that leads to stress and various physical and psychological health problems. Worrying consumes time, akin to sitting on a rocking chair and mistaking it for progress. Experience has shown that the future often turns out better than expected or not as dire as initially imagined. Our insistence on controlling outcomes fuels our worries. As discussed earlier, this is an unrealistic expectation. By embracing the Serenity Prayer, we must accept with serenity that the results of our efforts are not always within our control. However, since our minds tend to worry, we must reprogram them through thought conditioning and meditation. When action is required, let us take small steps mindfully, striving to do our best in any endeavour.

Practicing emptying our minds daily by engaging in prayers, affirmations, and meditation before sleep is an effective way to release worries. Scheduling a specific time slot in our day or week to address our concerns is also beneficial. When we notice a pattern of worrying thoughts, we can interrupt them by stopping, identifying what is troubling us, and writing it down in a "Worry Box-4 P.M. on Sunday." When we open the box at the designated time, we often find that many of the problems have either resolved themselves or no longer appear as daunting [18].

Another helpful technique is to note our worries and place them in a metaphorical "God's Worry Basket." Before going to bed each day, we can pray for guidance, wisdom, and strength to handle the problems contained in the basket [18]. By recognizing that we can only control our efforts and not the results, we can surrender the outcomes of our actions to a higher power. This relinquishment lightens our burdens and improves our effectiveness.

Acceptance

Unwanted situations or hurtful behaviour from others often lead to feelings of misery. Our typical response in such cases is to experience negative emotions such as worry, stress, anxiety, anger, or hatred. These emotions drain our energy, create unhappiness, and even impact our physical and psychological well-being. Moreover, they diminish our efficiency. Since these events are beyond our control and have already occurred, we must learn to accept them without fostering negativity. Instead, we should focus on what we can do under the given circumstances. Acceptance does not imply approval. Sometimes, the situation may be severe, making it challenging to avoid negative feelings. Rather than resisting such emotions, we can acknowledge and accept them. Doing so prevents emotional build-up that may lead to psychological and physical health problems. After identifying and accepting our feelings, we can sit with them peacefully for as long as necessary, allowing them to dissipate. If new emotions arise, we can repeat the acceptance process, embracing them with love and compassion.

It is crucial to make peace with our past and future. We cannot change the past; the future is uncertain and beyond our control. Dwelling on the past (good or bad) is akin to driving a car while fixating on the rear-view mirror. Similarly, fixating on the future (whether positive or negative) diverts our focus from the road ahead. Both behaviours are equally dangerous. The present moment demands our attention.

Nature teaches us valuable lessons about change. The world is constantly in flux, with some changes occurring cyclically, like day and night or the changing seasons. Other changes, such as storms and earthquakes, are less predictable. However, nature adapts to these changes effortlessly. We, too, must learn to adapt, as resistance to change leads to suffering.

We allow painful experiences to run their natural course if we view them as transient and fleeting. Just as these experiences arrive, they also depart naturally.

Finding humour in embarrassing situations can reduce their emotional intensity. Sharing and laughing about these moments with someone we trust can provide relief.

Forgiveness

We often hold onto memories of hurt or harm inflicted upon us by ourselves or others. However, harbouring resentment and anger harms us by robbing us of peace and potentially causing health problems. Therefore, forgiveness is not a favor we do for others but an act of self-care and well-being. It is equally important to forgive ourselves for our own mistakes. None of us is perfect; we are all on a journey of growth and self-improvement. Cultivating compassion and kindness towards others and ourselves fosters inner peace and happiness and enhances our work and relationships.

Positive Self-Talk and Visualization

Positive self-talk involves intentionally recalling our past accomplishments or those of our role models. By doing so, we provide our minds with a mental blueprint for future success. Visualization is an even more potent tool. Instead of merely thinking about past or future achievements, we visualize them in detail. Successful individuals in various domains of life widely use this technique. Engaging in positive self-talk and visualization boosts our confidence and self-image, which are essential for happiness and success. The seeds we plant today through these exercises may not yield immediate results, but the practice is more important. The habits we develop along the way hold more significance. As we might not always have external sources of motivation, fulfilling this need within ourselves is vital. These techniques serve the following purposes: training the mind and brain to align with our goals, reminding us of our purpose and motivating us by clarifying "what we are working on" and "why," improving self-confidence through preparedness for the future, and enhancing self-awareness by assessing our progress toward our goals.

Visualization also extends beyond positive self-talk. Let us visualize waking up feeling energized, peaceful, grateful, and happy. Likewise, let us imagine going to bed with a sense of happiness and gratitude. Praising our minds aids in their management.

We can visualize scenarios in the future that evoke fear and imagine ourselves calmly facing them, taking small steps toward overcoming them.

To counter self-criticism, such as "I am bored," "I am slow," or "I can't do this," we can reframe these thoughts by saying, "I am working on it" and "I am improving." Instead of believing "I can't do this," we should affirm, "I can do this by—," "I am learning," or "I am investing time to improve."

Showing ourselves self-compassion is crucial. When we feel worried, acknowledging those concerns and saying, "It's okay to feel this way. How can I help you through this?" can be powerful. Similarly, when feeling scared or worthless, offering encouragement such as, "I understand you feel scared, but you are strong and capable. You can handle this," or "Let's discuss what you love about yourself," can nurture self-compassion.

It is important to note that positive self-talk and visualization should be practiced when needed. Uncontrolled and obsessive engagement in these techniques can hinder focus and become a time-consuming distraction.

Diary of Achievements

What we focus on grows in our lives. Therefore, creating a treasury of our past achievements is invaluable. Let us compile a "Treasure Book of Our Accomplishments" encompassing various aspects of our lives, from childhood to the present. This collection should include anything that brings us joy and happiness. It does not necessarily require prizes or medals; any instance where we exceeded our expectations is worthy of inclusion. Once compiled, we should read at least one story before sleep or when our confidence wanes.

Peaceful Decision-Making

We often worry about making the right decisions in life. However, there is never a guarantee of correctness, as many factors are beyond our control. Moreover, our understanding of "right" or "wrong" decisions is flawed. Experience has shown that what may appear as the right decision at one point can turn into a disaster, and what may seem like a wrong decision can lead to unexpected success. Therefore, looking back at past decisions with hindsight offers little meaning. We cannot change so-called wrong decisions; we can only learn from them and apply those lessons in the future. Our maturity and wisdom influence our decision-making at a given moment, which constantly evolves. Accepting the inherent imperfection of decision-making is essential. The best way to improve our chances of making better decisions is to cultivate happiness and inner peace. In this state, our thinking becomes clear, allowing us to make balanced decisions while considering all relevant factors. In this state, we can tap into intuitive wisdom, which often surpasses logic and intellect. However, despite all these efforts, there are no guarantees of making the right decision, as the notion of right and wrong is subjective. Succumbing to indecision leads to procrastination, so it is crucial to develop the ability to make decisions and take ownership of them, bringing us peace.

The Importance of a Mentor

In Japan, a greeting asks whether you have met a wise person. They believe meeting such a person is like taking an elevator to higher levels instead of climbing stairs. Having good mentors is crucial in every aspect of life. Top athletes often have paid professionals as mentors. A good mentor is not only knowledgeable but also happy and successful, with a genuine desire to share their wisdom and empower others. To find mentors, we can start by praying to meet such individuals. We can also inquire and seek recommendations from others who may know of wise and experienced individuals. We may need different mentors at different stages of our journey, depending on what we aim to learn from them. We should express gratitude for their guidance and pray for their well-being.

The Three Types of Mentors

As Buddha neared the end of his life, a concerned disciple asked him how they should proceed after his passing. Buddha's response highlighted three types of mentors. The first and most desirable is an enlightened mentor, but finding such a mentor is challenging, and even if we are fortunate enough to encounter one, our time with them may be limited. The second-best option is to be in the company of like-minded individuals seeking self-improvement. Being part of such a group is highly beneficial in various ways. However, it may not always be feasible to find such a group. In such cases, we can turn to spiritual or self-help books that offer guidance and wisdom. These books provide a valuable resource over which we have complete control.

The next chapter will explore a powerful technique for cultivating a peaceful mind.

• • •

CHAPTER IV

Practice and Benefits of Meditation

"Meditation is not an evasion; it is a serene encounter with reality." - Thich Nhat Hanh.

What is Meditation?

In our pursuit of happiness, we often look outwardly, but Roman Emperor Marcus Aurelius wisely advised us to look within, as the foundation of all good lies there. Meditation is a powerful technique that allows us to do just that.

Negativity and unhappiness disrupt our minds, while positivity and happiness bring peace and tranquility. Meditation is the art of cultivating peace, harmony, and happiness within us.

Mindfulness, the ability to be fully present and aware of our thoughts and actions without judgment or excessive reactivity, plays a vital role in meditation. While mindfulness is crucial during seated meditation, it is equally valuable in our daily activities. The mind can become overwhelmed by external distractions and influences, leading to increased stress and reduced efficiency. Mindfulness keeps unnecessary thoughts at bay, providing rest for the mind and enhancing the effectiveness of our actions.

Mindfulness is useful everywhere. It is perhaps the most important thing ever to learn in life. Mindfulness is a source of happiness and joy.

Meditation, a practice with roots dating back thousands of years, has been utilized by spiritual practitioners to achieve peace, understand the self, and connect with a higher power. Athletes and military personnel have also harnessed meditation to gain an edge in their professions. However, its potential for enhancing the lives of ordinary individuals in all aspects remains relatively unknown. Thankfully, extensive research conducted over several decades has confirmed its benefits. Just as physical exercise improves our quality of life, mental exercise through meditation energizes us, instills peace and efficiency, enhances health, and makes us more attractive to others. It also positively transforms our professional, social, and personal lives. Meditation enhances concentration, cultivates relaxation and alertness, and fosters inner peace, mental clarity, and happiness [6]. We can comprehend its impact using the analogy of a pot of water with sediments. When the pot is stirred, the water appears murky, but when it is still, the sediments settle, and the water becomes clear.

Meditation aims to reduce stress and access happiness at will, regardless of external circumstances. It is achieved through self-awareness of our thoughts and emotions and understanding how and why we think and feel the way we do.

Types of Meditation

Meditation serves as a bridge between our conscious and subconscious minds. The meditative state should synchronize with our daily activities, fostering thoughtful and responsive living instead of defaulting to automatic reactions. Two forms of meditation are crucial and complement each other. The first is meditation in a state of rest and solitude, which most of us are familiar with. The second is meditation in action, where we mindfully engage with our surroundings and activities. This portable form of meditation allows us to remain calm even amidst distractions and holds immense utility as it requires no additional time or specific space. However, just as we learn to drive a car on quiet roads before venturing into heavier traffic, it is advisable to practice meditation at rest before attempting meditation in action.

Life inevitably presents us with challenges; meditation does not change that fact. However, it transforms our perspective, empowering us to skillfully navigate those challenges without sacrificing our dreams and ambitions. Meditation enables us to strive for our best and achieve our goals.

Thoughts and Emotions in Meditation

A common concern among beginners is the flood of thoughts that arise when they commence meditation and close their eyes. Thoughts are always present, whether we meditate or not. During our active engagements, we aren't aware of them. When we sit quietly, doing nothing, we become acutely aware of our thoughts. The purpose of meditation is to heighten our awareness of these thoughts. It is essential not to engage with or create stories around them, regardless of their content or quantity. If we find ourselves getting caught up in thoughts, it's perfectly okay. We gently return to the practice without feeling guilty. With consistent practice, such occurrences will naturally diminish, although it may take longer to settle the mind if we have had a particularly agitated day.

Managing thoughts is relatively easier than dealing with emotions, which often pose a challenge during meditation. However, emotional awareness is a vital aspect of meditation. Rather than becoming overwhelmed by emotions, we should observe them and allow the energy to pass through our bodies. Through practice, we gain insights into the triggers of our emotions and understand how they affect us physically. With continued meditation practice, we become more emotionally balanced individuals.

Breathing-Based Meditation

Breathing is an ever-present anchor to the present moment. We bring our minds into the here and now by directing our focus to the breath. All our experiences, challenges, and responses also exist in the present moment. We know that our breath frequency is related to our thoughts' frequency. When we are disturbed, our breathing and thoughts become rapid, slowing down when we are at peace. Focusing on the breath alleviates suffering caused by distressing thoughts or physical discomfort.

Lucas Rockwood aptly states, *"Change your breathing, change your life."* Dr. Andrew Weil, author of "Breathing: The Master Key to Self-Healing," suggests that conscious regulation of breathing is the most efficient technique for relaxation [19]. Without attempting to alter it, redirecting our attention to the breath leads us toward a state of relaxation. Shallow breathing, a stress response, further perpetuates stress. To break this cycle, we can take a few deep breaths, even amidst our busy daily routines, initiating an upward spiral of deep breathing and calm. It can be done anytime and anywhere, shifting our minds from fight-or-flight mode to a relaxation response. Tal-Ben Shahar offers a modified technique involving three steps [1]: mindful deep breaths, focusing on the day's purpose or life, and expressing gratitude. This practice combines the physiological benefits of deep breathing with the cognitive benefits of focusing on something positive, proving highly effective in cultivating peacefulness when repeated several times throughout the day.

Our autonomic nervous system comprises The Sympathetic Nervous System (SNS) and the Parasympathetic Nervous System (PSNS). The SNS activates the fight-or-flight response in the face of perceived threats, while the PSNS acts as a calming mechanism for the mind and body. Mindful, deep breathing decreases heart rate and cortisol levels, stimulating the PSNS and reducing stress.

Mantra Chanting Meditation

Many individuals are unaware of the benefits associated with this form of meditation. Those with religious inclinations often practice mantra chanting, as it involves the repetition of a sacred phrase or sound. It can be done seated or during activities such as walking, driving, or even lying down. Chanting a mantra, either silently or audibly (preferably only audible to ourselves), a few times can be a powerful practice. It is important to chant the mantra slowly, allowing us to focus on its meaning. Due to the emotional connection with the higher power associated with the mantra, additional benefits, such as a sense of protection, are experienced.

Chanting a mantra for a few minutes before sleep brings a sense of lightness and improves sleep quality. Simply listening to a recorded mantra can also be highly beneficial. Before sleep, listening to a Peace mantra (Shanti Mantra), where we pray for the well-being of everyone, can be especially helpful. The sound of the mantra should be just audible to us.

I have been practicing both forms of meditation for over 40 years, and I have found great enjoyment in mantra meditation during long drives alone.

Benefits of Meditation

Scientific research conducted by neuroscientists has revealed the profound benefits of meditation on our brains. Years of consistent meditation practice have been shown to increase the thickness of the left prefrontal cortex, the area responsible for generating happiness. A study at the

University of Montreal demonstrated that meditators had significantly thicker brain regions associated with pain regulation and emotions, reducing their intensity [20]. Even just five minutes of mindful breathing can initiate these benefits, making it one of the most potent interventions for happiness. Studies have indicated that individuals experience calmness, contentment, heightened awareness, and empathy after a short meditation session. Long-term meditation practice results in permanent rewiring of the brain, elevating happiness levels, reducing stress, and enhancing immunity. Research has also shown that meditation increases brain activity in regions associated with optimism and positive thinking. Beginning with just five minutes daily is a commendable start [2].

Randomized studies have found that meditation surpasses medication in preventing depression relapse. Within six months, 75% of mindfulness practitioners could discontinue medication and were less likely to relapse [20]. While medication plays an important role, a comparative analysis of 39 studies conducted by researchers at Boston University emphasized the far-reaching benefits of mindfulness training. Meditation empowers individuals to cope better with difficulties in general.

A lead neuroscientist researcher at the University of Pennsylvania studied the effects of mindfulness on US Marines and stated, *"Building mind fitness with mindfulness training can help anyone who must maintain peak performance in the face of extremely stressful circumstances."* Meditation has been shown to reduce the time it takes to fall asleep by half. Several studies based on mindfulness practices have reported significant improvements in cognitive skills after just four training days. Participants performed exceptionally well in tasks requiring sustained physical and mental attention, even under stressful, time-constrained conditions [20].

Mindfulness practice decreases the intensity of negative emotions and reduces anxiety. A study conducted at the University of Massachusetts Medical School found that 90% of participants experienced a significant reduction in anxiety and depression after eight weeks of mindfulness training. Remarkably, these benefits were maintained even three years later [20]. Additionally, experiments have demonstrated that a mere ten minutes of meditation can significantly improve GRE scores, enhance decision-making, and prevent impulsive mistakes. Even just ninety seconds of slow, deep breathing can lead to substantial spikes in happiness.

When I looked at ways to improve qualities required for success, like intelligence, motivation, will power, discipline, and concentration, I was surprised to see that meditation does it all.

Slow, deep breathing helps the body through increased Oxygen intake and the mind through thought reduction.

Meditation at Rest

Meditation at rest involves focusing inward to understand the self and connect with the wellspring of wisdom within. It is ideally practiced on an empty stomach at a specific time, such as early morning or evening. Choosing a quiet space with minimal distractions, dim lighting, and preferably fresh air is best. Sit with your spine erect, cross-legged on the floor with a mat or on a chair. Close your eyes to shut out visual distractions, and if comfortable, use headphones to minimize auditory disturbances. The meditation process itself revolves around slow, deep, mindful breathing.

Numerous guided meditation variants can be found online,

allowing you to explore and choose the one that resonates most with you. During meditation, we observe the breath entering and exiting through the nostrils, paying attention to our shoulders, chest, and diaphragm movements. It is crucial to maintain a comfortable and steady breathing rhythm. Don't worry if your mind wanders during practice; this is natural due to the nature of the mind. When you notice a wandering thought, simply acknowledge it without judgment and gently redirect your focus back to the breath. Initially, the mind may frequently wander, but with consistent practice, these instances will become less frequent. In terms of the flow of thoughts, an apt analogy for the mind during different stages of meditation is that it may resemble a rapid waterfall, a fast-flowing river, a slow-moving river, and eventually, a tranquil lake.

To enhance concentration during meditation, you can silently repeat phrases such as "I am breathing in" and "I am breathing out" or use the words "in" and "out." When you are engaged in saying something specific, it becomes more difficult for distracting thoughts to arise. Counting is another effective method for improving concentration, as it prevents the mind from wandering. One can even mantra chanting instead of counting.

The duration of meditation should always be based on your comfort level. Beginners can start with just a few minutes and gradually increase the duration. Practicing meditation for ten to fifteen minutes regularly is recommended for sustained benefits. On days when you're pressed for time or not feeling well, even meditating for three minutes ensures that the habit remains intact.

Imagine holding a glass of water. It is not the weight of the glass and water that tires us but the time we hold it. Holding it for a short while is manageable, but holding it for an extended period can lead to hand fatigue. The same principle applies to the stress caused by life's problems. Learning to let go of that stress before sleeping through meditation at the end of the day is essential. Engaging in this practice more frequently is even better. During lunch or tea breaks, taking just two to three minutes for mindful, deep breathing can provide quick stress relief. It can be done discreetly in various settings, such as classrooms, exam halls, or during meetings, without drawing attention. You will enjoy the feeling of relaxation, and others will appreciate your peaceful demeanor.

Balanced Breathing

Breathe in while counting from one to four, and breathe out while counting from one to four. This technique can be practiced anywhere and anytime to maintain a calm and focused mind.

For Better Sleep

When lying down in bed, relax your body. Breathe in for a count of four and breathe out for a count of four. You can repeat this ten times or continue until you fall asleep.

Deep Relaxation

This practice allows the body to rest, heal, and rejuvenate. Begin by relaxing the body and directing your attention to each body part, sending love and care.

Guide your awareness to your hair, scalp, brain, ears, neck, lungs, internal organs, digestive system, pelvis, and other parts needing healing, embracing, and sending love and care.

If you have only a few minutes for relaxation, focus on the body part that feels most stressed. For example, if you have been working on digital screens for an extended period, take a few moments to relax your eyes. Sit in a relaxed position, close your eyes, and bring your awareness to your eyes. Relax your eyes and express love and gratitude towards them. After a few minutes of conscious breathing, you can silently say, "I am aware of my eyes" while breathing in, and "I smile at my eyes" while breathing out.

For a full-body deep relaxation session, allocate at least twenty minutes. Lie down on a comfortable mattress with your hands resting by your sides. Become aware of the floor and the sensations of your body contacting it. Allow your body to sink into the mattress. Engage in conscious breathing for a few minutes, then direct your attention to your abdomen, noticing its rise and fall. Bring awareness to your eyes, relax them, and express love and gratitude.

Next, repeat the relaxation exercise for each body part, starting with the shoulders, arms (upper and lower), wrists, hands, and fingers. Proceed to focus on the heart, followed by the legs (thighs, knees, calves, ankles, feet, and toes). As you go through each body part, imagine your entire body feeling like a lily floating on water or a free cloud drifting through the sky.

Meditation Experiences

In my early twenties, I faced various health problems and turned to yoga and breathing exercises for relief. These practices helped alleviate my nasal blockages and respiratory issues caused by allergies and brought a sense of calm and tranquility. My spiritual practice of mantra chanting meditation for over four decades has also profoundly impacted my well-being.

Shinzen Young, a meditation expert, shared his experience of overcoming weakness in math through meditation. Despite struggling with math throughout his schooling, he used meditation to master the subject, surprising himself and others [4].

Chade-Meng Tan, a former Google engineer and author,

discovered how meditation transformed his life and earned him the nickname "A jolly good fellow" among his colleagues. His "Search Inside Yourself" meditation program gained popularity and has helped numerous individuals [3].

Late Mr. B. P. Bam, a retired police commissioner and sports enthusiast, found relief from severe back pain through Indian yoga and meditation practices. He recovered and applied these techniques to his sports activities without surgery or medication. His remarkable improvements caught professional athletes' attention, and he became a renowned sports coach, working with individuals like Rahul Dravid [22].

Throughout my research for this book, I have encountered many authors who are avid meditators and numerous students, colleagues, and professionals who have experienced significant benefits from meditation practice.

Meditation in Action

As mentioned earlier, extending the meditative state into our daily activities is important by practicing mindfulness. Here are some examples of incorporating mindfulness into different aspects of life.

Mindful Social Interactions

Extending mindfulness to personal interactions involves listening, observing, and responding sensitively. It cultivates social intelligence and fosters better relationships in various settings, be it at home, work, or with friends.

Mindful listening plays a crucial role in building connections. By giving our full attention to the person speaking without interruptions, nodding, or using affirming phrases like "I see," we show our genuine interest and make others feel valued.

Mindfulness in Intense Activities

The benefits of mindfulness are most pronounced during intense activities when stress levels are high. For example, being mindful during a class lecture or study session allows for open, non-judgmental attention, leading to better understanding. This practice remains effective even in challenging academic situations or exams, where mindfulness lets us stay calm and perform to the best of our abilities.

Mindful Morning Chores

Incorporating mindfulness into morning routines can enhance the overall experience and set a positive tone for the day. While looking at oneself in the mirror, offering a loving smile and saying, "Good morning (your name), I love you as you are," cultivates self-acceptance. Paying attention to the small details during activities like brushing teeth or taking a shower, such as the condition of the toothbrush bristles, the texture of the toothpaste, or the aroma of soap, helps us fully engage with the present moment. Expressing gratitude and love towards our body during these routines further promotes well-being.

Mindful Meals

We can extend mindfulness during meals by expressing gratitude towards those involved in meal preparation and delivery. Paying attention to the food's taste, appearance, and details and maintaining a relaxed smile throughout the meal helps us fully savor the experience.

Mindful Walks

During mindful walks, we can focus on the movement of our feet and the sensation of touching the ground. Being aware of the surrounding environment, such as feeling the touch of air on our skin, noticing the warmth of the sun or the softness of shade, and appreciating the colors, shapes, smells, and sensations around us, helps us connect with the present moment. We can also engage with nature by touching tree trunks, leaves, and flowers and observing their features.

Meditation for Tension Release

To release physical tension in any body part, we can shift our focus to that area, breathe into it, and consciously release it. As we let go, we can affirm silently, relieving ourselves of strain and inviting a sense of calmness and tranquility.

Meditation to Overcome Fear

When fear overwhelms us, we can practice a breathing technique to alleviate its grip. Inhale for a count of four, hold your breath for a count of four, and exhale for a count of four. Repeat this cycle until we begin to feel better [17].

Quick Happiness Meditations

Two brief meditations can generate happiness. The "loving-kindness" meditation takes just fifteen seconds and can be practiced even in a classroom. Simply look at someone and sincerely say, "I wish you happiness. I wish you happiness." This practice can be extended to random individuals outside or even imagined friends [3].

Professor Barbara Fredrickson conducted a study within an organization where participants engaged in loving-kindness meditation for themselves or others for 20 minutes daily. Over seven weeks, the participants reported decreased anxiety and depression, increased joy and happiness, improved physical health, enhanced relationships, and a heightened sense of purpose.

The "loving compassion" meditation takes just fifteen seconds and can be done anywhere. It involves expressing a compassionate wish for someone suffering from illness or poor performance by saying, "I wish you to be free from suffering. I wish you to be free from suffering" [3].

Meditation to Improve Resilience

For four minutes, recall a memory of failure, but instead of immersing ourselves in the emotions, observe them as a third person without judgment. By practicing emotional intelligence in this way, we become familiar with the emotions and can take conscious steps to prevent their unconscious amplification in similar situations [4].

Tips for Cultivating Regularity in Mindfulness Meditation

It is important to cultivate regularity in meditation practice. At the start of each day, affirming our intention to be as mindful as possible in every task, conversation, and meeting sets a positive tone. Throughout the day, using mindfulness reminders, such as periodic alerts or triggers like washroom breaks, drink breaks, phone notifications, or email messages, can help us maintain mindfulness amidst a busy schedule. Using the initials "MF" in our frequently used passwords can be an additional reminder.

The next chapter delves into the critical importance of self-awareness in enhancing happiness and success.

• • •

CHAPTER V

Self-Awareness: A Key to Personal Growth

"Knowing yourself is the beginning of all wisdom." - Aristotle

Understanding Self-Awareness

Good vision is essential to function effectively in various aspects of our lives, such as at work, home, and on the road. Similarly, self-awareness acts as our inner vision. Without it, our effectiveness and happiness are diminished, and we may make mistakes in major life decisions.

To be happy and successful, we need to be continuously alert. Self-awareness does that.

Our natural inclination is to engage with the external world through our senses. This lifelong pursuit of observing and experiencing the world is crucial for deriving maximum benefits. However, we often overlook that all our external observations can be seriously flawed if we are unaware of ourselves. Unfortunately, most of us find ourselves in this state because our education system and upbringing primarily focus on the external world. Therefore, we must develop the critical skill of looking within.

The Power of Questions

Questions serve as powerful tools for focusing our consciousness and determining our actions. The key to self-awareness lies in asking ourselves meaningful questions. A fulfilling life arises from our ability to ask quality questions [5].

Asking important and appropriate questions is a vital skill

to learn. We need not worry about not having all the answers. There are various resources available to help us find answers, including internet searches and seeking guidance from mentors. The habit of questioning ourselves is what matters. Asking questions redirects our focus from everything else to the specific inquiry. Questions also lead us to resources to help us solve problems [5].

By posing genuine questions, we challenge our assumptions and conventional thinking about what is possible in our lives.

The Benefits of Self-Awareness

We often ask acquaintances how they are doing as a social convention without genuine curiosity. However, when it comes to our loved ones, we sincerely inquire about their well-being. As discussed in Chapter 2, we are the most important person in our own lives. Loving ourselves means regularly checking in on our well-being. We must pay attention to the continuous self-talk happening within us. Becoming aware of our attitudes toward ourselves with kindness and curiosity is valuable. We can achieve this through deliberate and loving self-talk, like communicating with our best friend or grandmother. This inner dialogue helps us assess our current situation and, through deeper introspection, discover ways to improve it.

Observability is a crucial prerequisite for control. We cannot hit a target we cannot see. However, observability alone does not guarantee control. Therefore, self-awareness is a prerequisite for self-improvement. It encompasses various aspects of our inner selves. Self-awareness makes us more proactive and enhances self-confidence, self-acceptance, and self-esteem. It improves decision-making and communication skills, making us more successful in our careers and relationships.

How to Cultivate Self-Awareness?

To become self-aware, we need to focus on the following aspects: our aspirations (goals and desires), worries, fears, emotions, and their triggers, habits, beliefs, values, thought patterns, attitude, self-esteem, character, principles, time management, the company we keep, and whether it contributes to our success and happiness. It's essential to address these aspects individually, as many take time to uncover, requiring patience. Mark Manson [15] compares this process to peeling an onion, where there are multiple layers to explore. Long-term self-awareness activities can be dedicated to weekends or holidays. Once we understand these aspects, we can shift to monthly reviews instead of weekly ones. However, some elements, such as recognizing our feelings, should be done daily and hourly.

While some individuals understand the importance of self-awareness and attempt self-inquiry, it often doesn't yield significant results because they try to keep it all in their minds without writing down important points in a journal. Thoughts stored only in our minds are like volatile memories, whereas a journal acts as a recorded memory like a hard disk. Without a record and review system, improvement tends to be short-lived. Therefore, it is crucial to take notes in a journal or using digital devices like laptops or mobile phones as part of this practice. Traditional and modern systems have advantages and disadvantages, so choose the most comfortable. However, ensure that your data is safely stored and organized. Adopting a systematic and robust approach is essential to reap the benefits of self-awareness.

One common reason why many people avoid self-awareness practices is the belief that the time and effort required for improvement are beyond their capabilities.

However, this should not discourage us because improvement can happen gradually, with a focus on the present moment.

Honesty and understanding are essential for effective introspection.

Journaling: Unveiling Your Thoughts

Writing is valuable for creating a record that proves extremely useful later. It clarifies various aspects of our thinking and emotions, making it easier to improve our lives.

In a study involving a group of laid-off professionals, participants were asked to write about their feelings for twenty-five minutes each day for five days. Most found new jobs much faster than those who didn't engage in this exercise. After eight months, 68.4 percent of the former category had secured employment, compared to 27.3 percent in the latter category.

A study at the University of Texas [3] involved students writing about their most meaningful personal experiences for 15 minutes over several consecutive days. The students not only felt better but also achieved better grades. A similar finding emerged from a study at Missouri University, where even a few minutes of writing proved beneficial.

Angela Duckworth [23] suggests asking self-awareness questions such as: "What do I like to think about?" "Where does my mind wander?" "What matters most to me?" "How do I enjoy spending my time?" "What do I find unbearable?"

Here are some other questions: "Am I happy at work? How can I become happier? What can I do to make my work more enjoyable?" "What are my fears? How do they affect me?"

Make a list of all your desires. Then, take a few minutes to focus on each desire individually to understand better why you have that desire.

Meditation for Self-Awareness

One of the least understood benefits of meditation is its ability to increase self-awareness. During meditation, emotions, beliefs, and thought patterns often surface. Chade-Meng Tan suggests the following exercise to promote inner peace:

First, be peaceful by mindful deep breathing for a few minutes. Then, take three minutes to reflect on your current feelings. Write down "What I'm feeling right now is..." and allow yourself to freely express your emotions on paper. If you initially have nothing to write, simply jot down "Nothing to write" and continue until something comes to mind [3].

To explore different facets of your thinking, use the following prompts individually for two minutes each [3]. Choose a couple of random prompts each day:

- "What hurts me is..."
- "What motivates me is..."
- "I am inspired by..."
- "Today, I aspire to..."
- "Things that give me pleasure are..."
- "My strengths are..."
- "Things that annoy me are..."
- "My weaknesses are..."

You can apply a similar approach to explore motivation, inspiration, strengths, weaknesses, worries, and anger.

Before going to sleep each day, take a moment to ask yourself simple questions such as, "Was I happier today?" and "Did I make progress towards my main goal today?" Respond with a simple "Yes" or "No" and record your reasons in a journal. This practice lets you track your daily, weekly, and monthly trends. It helps you identify whether negative trends are mere blips or causes for concern. It also prompts you to contemplate the causes and potential solutions.

Emotional Intelligence (E.I.)

Previously, intellect was considered the primary factor in success [3]. However, research has shown that Emotional Intelligence is also a significant factor. It begins with being aware of our emotions. Through journaling exercises, we can identify the emotions we experience and the triggers that make us happy or unhappy. By reflecting on a happy or sad event and observing its slow-motion impact on our bodies, we can better understand the waxing and waning of emotions. This awareness empowers us to control reactive automatic processes often accompanying negative emotions. Emotions can become valuable feedback for improvement when we view them as friends.

We should explore why we experience certain emotions. These inquiries illuminate our definitions of success and failure, helping us understand the root causes of overwhelming emotions. This understanding enables us to act and make changes.

Emotional intelligence begins with recognizing that we are experiencing an emotion, both mentally and physically. The physical response to emotions is akin to a slow-motion replay of the mental experience. Therefore, it becomes easier to observe and understand the stages of emotion: arising, intensifying, subsiding, and dissipating. Through non-judgmental observation, we allow emotional energy to flow out of our bodies. More importantly, we observe how these emotions impact our bodies throughout the process. As replicating real-life environments for this practice can be challenging; we simulate it briefly. It involves first attaining peace through a few minutes of deep, mindful breathing. Then, we recall positive or negative memories one at a time, mindfully experiencing the complete emotional process within our bodies. By comprehending how each emotion affects us and identifying its triggers, we can prevent the recurrence of negative emotions or respond to them more effectively. This understanding helps us learn from our failures and minimize their adverse effects, fostering resilience.

Studies have shown that Emotional Intelligence (E.I.) is one of the best predictors of success at work and fulfilment in life. It enhances our initiative to tackle challenges and boosts self-confidence. Developing E.I. enables us to exceed our perceived capabilities.

Discover Your Beliefs

Take some time to list your beliefs about yourself and others. Assess whether these beliefs empower or disempower you. If any beliefs are limiting, question their accuracy by examining the evidence supporting them. This deliberate exercise allows you to shift your mindset from fixed to growth, scarcity to abundance, and pessimism to optimism.

Discover Your Values

Explore your values and arrange them in order of priority, from most important to least important. Assess whether these values are beneficial or detrimental to your well-being. Continuously review whether your life is improving or if any conflicts are causing stress. In such cases, reassess and reorder your priorities by adding or removing values from your list.

Assessing Your Stress Levels

Stress and happiness share an inverse relationship, making it valuable to gauge your stress levels. You can choose one of the answers given against each question. You may modify the choices if you wish.

1. Do you possess a deep sense of self-love and self-respect? Answers: Never, sometimes, most of the times, always.
2. Do you feel deserving of love and affection from others? Answers: Never, sometimes, most of the times, always.
3. How was your thought process today; primarily positive or negative? Answers: Mostly negative, sometimes negative, mostly positive.
4. Do you hold others responsible for your current circumstances? Answers: Most of the times, sometimes, rarely.
5. Are the people around you supportive and trustworthy? Answers: Never, sometimes, most of the times, always.
6. Do you maintain confidence in the potential for a brighter future? Answers: Never, sometimes, most of the times, always.
7. Do you feel that you lack sufficient time for essential tasks? Answers: Always, most of the times, sometimes, rarely.
8. Does the prospect of competition intimidate you? Answers: Never, sometimes, most of the times, always.
9. Do you believe in your ability to enhance your skills in any area you choose? Answers: Always, most of the times, sometimes, rarely.
    Remember, even if your stress level isn't ideal, there's no need for concern. This exercise is simply a means of self-awareness. The goal of this book is to demonstrate how you can enhance your well-being and personal growth.

Recovering from Stress

Identifying and expressing our feelings through writing is one of the quickest ways to recover from stress. Brain scans of stressed individuals show that describing their emotions in a journal or sharing them with a friend or colleague immediately diminishes the intensity of these emotions, leading to improved well-being and enhanced decision-making skills.

During times of stress, we can identify the aspects of the situation that are within our control and those that are not. By pinpointing one small goal we can accomplish, we regain a feeling of control and resilience.

The next chapter will explore the important role of prayers in fostering happiness.

• • •

CHAPTER VI

Prayer: A Tool for Success and Harmony

"Prayer is man's greatest power." - W. Clement Stone.

Understanding Prayer

Prayer is often misunderstood and carries various biases. To grasp its true essence, let us first explore what prayer entails.

Even individuals who have achieved success face worries, insecurities, and stress stemming from factors like competition-related pressure, personal or family health issues, relationship struggles, or breakups. Tragically, I have encountered brilliant and accomplished students who have resorted to or contemplated suicide due to failed relationships. Many students' academic journeys have been derailed by their inability to cope with such setbacks.

As discussed in earlier chapters, sharing our problems with a trustworthy person and seeking wise counsel can help us find solace. This person could be a family member, mentor, or friend. However, they may not always be available, and there may be certain matters we cannot share with anyone. This is where engaging in a dialogue with an imaginary higher power can be immensely helpful in alleviating stress and making better decisions. This dialogue, known as prayer, is not solely about making requests. Prayers can serve as a release valve for pressure or act as a spare tire, crucial in times of crisis. However, prayer is a more powerful tool than simply an emergency resource.

Prayer is a deeply personal experience that holds different

meanings for us. In general, it involves a dialogue encompassing conversation, devotion, requests, praise, or expressions of gratitude directed towards an object of worship, such as God or universal power. Even those who do not believe in God, like Buddhists and Jains, engage in prayer. We often pray for ourselves and then extend our prayers to our loved ones. Wishing good things for others is also a form of prayer, and even atheists unknowingly participate in it. Some of the best prayers, like the Universal Peace Prayer (Shanti mantra), do not involve any higher power; they are just expressions of goodwill for all.

Prayer for well-being is like a candlelight in the dark world.

The Potential of Prayer

As mentioned earlier, engaging in a dialogue with a higher power whenever we need support is a form of prayer that reduces stress. When we establish a constant connection with this higher power, we are less likely to engage in harmful behavior or actions that could harm others or ourselves. Such behaviors may include addiction to drugs or digital devices and neglecting long-term goals to pursue short-term pleasures.

While we frequently pray for small and significant things, we gradually learn through experience that many prayers remain unanswered. It is akin to requesting something from our parents, fully aware that they may not grant all our wishes. We also learn that we must put in the effort to achieve success. Since each of us is unique, our prayers also reflect our individuality. Instead of relying solely on prayers to fulfill our desires, exploring an alternative and rational approach is worth exploring.

Imagine asking for a fish; it may feed us for one day. However, if we are taught how to catch a fish, we can provide for our family for a lifetime. Instead of praying solely for success in our endeavors, we can pray for assistance in developing positive qualities that increase the likelihood of success. Once we possess these qualities, they remain with us throughout our lives. Prayer does not necessarily alter challenging circumstances or change the behavior of difficult individuals. Rather, it transforms us, enabling us to respond to these situations and people more effectively.

Most of us possess a limited understanding of the potential power of prayer. As a result, we tend to pray only at home in the morning or evening, often as a mechanical ritual driven by fear of God rather than love for Him. We also resort to prayer during emergencies. However, we rarely integrate prayer into our daily activities, where its maximum benefits lie. Our ability to think and act rationally becomes impaired when we are distressed. Therefore, without proper training in prayer, our prayers may prove ineffective during difficult times.

Faith and harmony play essential roles in the prayer process. The strength of our prayers depends on the depth of our faith in the higher power, while harmony facilitates effective communication. Group prayers hold even greater potency than individual ones, as personal vibrations multiply through a resonating effect. All religions encourage group prayers in various settings, such as homes, temples, churches, gurudwaras, and mosques.

Research on Prayer

Research consistently demonstrates the benefits of prayer on physical, mental, and emotional well-being. For instance, prayer provides solace when experiencing pain, loss, or traumatic events. It instills hope and offers strong motivation for achieving our goals. Prayer also fosters a sense of concern for the well-being of others. Even in seemingly hopeless situations where taking action seems impossible, prayer allows us to find peace by surrendering to higher powers.

Dr. Rosmarin, Assistant Professor of Psychology at Harvard Medical School and Director of Spirituality and Mental Health at McLean Hospital in Belmont, researched prayer [24]. The findings suggest that prayer can yield benefits like those of meditation. It calms the nervous system, preventing the fight-or-flight response in stressful situations. Prayer enables us to become less reactive to negative emotions.

According to Amy Wachholtz, Associate Professor of Clinical Health Psychology and Director at the University of Colorado, Denver, those who pray to a higher power often describe the effect as unburdening oneself from carrying a heavy backpack for an extended period [24].

Swami Vivekananda was once asked what he gained from prayers. He said: *"I gained nothing. In fact, I lost anger, depression, jealousy, irritation, and insecurity."*

Determining the Right Prayer Time

Prayer is a valuable technique for personal growth that can be practiced at any time and always proves beneficial. However, the best results are often obtained when drowsy, just before falling asleep. During this time, our analytical and conscious mind is less active, allowing prayers to reach our subconscious with minimal resistance. Another favorable time for prayer is immediately upon waking while still in bed. Our minds are fresh and highly receptive at this moment. Incorporating short prayers throughout the day, such as before starting a new activity or during bathroom breaks, proves highly effective in curbing the build-up of stress. These brief prayers take no more than fifteen seconds, yet their benefits are enormous. Before offering prayers, we must relax our minds through a few deep breaths. Simply closing our eyes and feeling the grace of God is also a powerful practice.

Who Should We Pray for?

Initially, let us offer prayers for the well-being, love, harmony, and happiness of everyone in the world, as exemplified in the Peace Prayer (Shanti Mantra). Additionally, we should pray for the welfare of those who have hurt us and, finally, for our near and dear ones. These acts of prayer are primarily for our peace and happiness. We can also extend our prayers to strangers while walking, driving, or utilizing any mode of transportation. We can pray for a harmonious encounter before it begins. When we anticipate hostility from a particular person, we can pray for their welfare and establish harmonious interactions.

When uncertain about the best course of action, let us meditate and pray for clarity and guidance with love and conviction. It is important not to impose strict timeframes or specific expectations on the advice we receive. By consistently practicing this, guidance will manifest in some form at the right moment.

Before delivering a speech or attending a meeting, we can pray for the well-being of the individuals present. Praying for those in the audience with whom we strongly disagree is always a beneficial strategy. It may not change the person, but it gives us calm. Subsequently, we can pray for a harmonious and successful event. While it may not directly impact others, from my extensive personal experience, I can confidently say that we always benefit by cultivating inner peace through this practice.

Personal Prayer Experiences

I have experienced tremendous benefits by incorporating

the abovementioned prayer practices into my life. Prayer has provided me with solace during distress and helped me make better decisions. By developing a deeper connection with the higher power, I have found strength and resilience in facing challenges. Prayer has guided me toward positive qualities and helped me focus on my long-term goals. Through prayer, I have discovered inner peace and the ability to respond to difficult situations gracefully.

My wife and I have experienced remarkable benefits through daily dialogues with God and our Guru. We share our joys, sorrows, worries, troubles, and even routine matters with them. These conversations encompass various aspects of our lives, including professions, finances, and relationships. Prayer has consistently brought us peace, enabling us to fulfil our duties effectively.

Allow me to share a couple of experiences, presenting them as factual events for your interpretation:

One instance involved a Ph.D. student supervised by my wife. The student had submitted his thesis for evaluation, and an examiner from India, who happened to be present at her Centre for another student's examination, revealed that he intended to reject the thesis due to the absence of mathematical modelling. Despite mathematical modelling not being within the student's or my wife's research area, the examiner expressed his dissatisfaction. The rejection of a Ph.D. thesis can be devastating for a student. When my wife informed me about this situation, we perceived that the examiner's actions stemmed from bitterness caused by retirement issues. Consequently, we prayed for peace and happiness for the examiner and his family. Surprisingly, the very next day, the examiner wrote to my wife, stating that he had approved the thesis without any adverse comments. Another experience involved a part-time Ph.D. student of my wife's who received warnings regarding unsatisfactory work. Eventually, my wife had to recommend the termination of the student's registration. In response, the student threatened to tarnish my wife's reputation and make her life miserable by lodging false complaints with the administration. Upon learning about the situation, we once again sensed that the student's vindictive intentions were rooted in unhappiness and frustration in his own life. We decided to pray fervently for his peace and happiness. To our surprise, the next day, the student informed my wife that he had decided against his initial plans and apologized for his behavior. He attributed his change of heart to his mother, who scolded him for his foolish intentions and reminded him of how his supervisor had been like a mother figure.

Examples of Prayers

Here are some examples of prayers that can be adapted to suit specific situations:

Universal Well-being Prayer: May everyone experience happiness and be free from illness. May all encounter auspicious circumstances. May no one suffer. Peace, peace, peace!

Peace: May there be peace surrounding me.

Finding the Right Mentors: Please guide me toward the right mentors to help me improve.

Friendships: Grant me the gift of discernment to recognize wise friends. Please teach me how to be a good friend.

Enhancing Productivity: God, assist me in being productive in my studies. Also, please enable me to make the best use of my time and approach my studies with utmost dedication.

Academic Success: God, help me focus on my books and notes. Please protect me from distractions, allowing me to maximize my time and comprehend my study subjects. Please grant me the ability to retain the knowledge when I need it.

Exams: God, support me in every test. Help me recall everything I have studied. Please grant me the calmness, focus, and confidence to perform to the best of my abilities. In the upcoming chapter, we will delve into the significant role of affirmations in fostering happiness and success.

• • •

CHAPTER VII

Affirmations: Rewiring Brain for Happiness and Success

"It's the repetition of affirmations that leads to belief, and once that belief becomes a deep conviction, things begin to happen." – Claude M. Bristol

Affirmations are often underestimated, yet they hold tremendous potential for personal improvement. They are simple word or phrase intentions that can empower us to improve our lives. Affirmations are the best form of self-talk and, when done correctly, become the most powerful tool for self-improvement. The beauty of affirmations is that they are not limited to religious beliefs and can be used by anyone, including atheists.

Affirmations are a strong mind programming technique to cultivate a happy attitude and positive thoughts. By repeating these autosuggestions, they get deeply embedded in our subconscious mind. In doing so, we replace harmful programs recorded in our default auto-pilot mode without conscious realization. Affirmations significantly improve our self-esteem, confidence, and overall mood.

When we use affirmations, we create a positive self-identity that enables us to handle difficult situations more effectively. It's important to note that we don't need to be exceptional, perfect, or excellent in life. Instead, we should strive to feel competent and equipped in the areas of life that hold personal value to us.

Within each of us, there exists a mixture of positive and negative qualities. The dominance of one over the other is often influenced by the conditioning of the mind, typically in an unconscious manner. Through the practice of positive affirmations, we consciously choose to take control of our lives by focusing on the positive aspects. It is crucial to frequently remind ourselves of our divine qualities by affirming statements such as "I am a divine soul," "I am a peaceful soul," "I am a happy soul," "I am a pure soul," and "I am a powerful soul."

To foster harmonious relationships with others, affirming similar positive qualities for the people who matter most to us is beneficial. By doing so, we contribute to their well-being and strengthen our connections.

Kamal Ravikant, an author and entrepreneur, shares his transformational journey of healing and personal growth through self-love affirmations [8]. Other books [9, 11] also provide numerous accounts of similar positive changes achieved through the power of affirmations. These real-life examples highlight the effectiveness of affirmations in improving various aspects of our lives.

Let me share an example from my personal life. My wife decided to pursue her Ph.D. after a significant gap due to marriage and raising children. She noticed a decline in her once-sharp memory during her initial literature survey. The first thing she did was adopt the following affirmation: "My memory is wonderful." Over time, she regained confidence in her memory and experienced a notable improvement.

To begin practicing affirmations, choosing an area of our life that we want to focus on for improvement is best. Then, select a few appropriate affirmations and repeat them every morning and evening. By starting our day with a positive outlook and ending it with a positive thought, we set ourselves up for success.

Affirmations also serve as a commitment to overcome obstacles. We take the first step toward achieving our goals by affirming that we will reach a specific destination. However, doubts can hinder the effectiveness of affirmations. It is crucial to align our emotions with our positive affirmations. Alongside affirmations, our actions throughout the day play a significant role. Affirmations are like seeds; they require a nurturing environment of positive thoughts to grow.

MRI studies have shown that affirmations build mental muscles and create neural pathways in areas responsible for optimism, such as the ventromedial prefrontal cortex [34]. Psychologists and medical professionals have conducted research confirming the benefits of affirmations.

Now, let's discuss how to perform affirmations effectively. The following guidelines will help you maximize the impact of your affirmations:

1. Affirmations should be positive, phrased in the present tense, and repeated with the belief that they are already true. Dr. Schecter suggests using short, actionable statements containing "I" and projecting a better future. For example, instead of saying, "I will achieve this goal and be happier and more fulfilled," rephrase it as "I am achieving this goal and becoming happier and more fulfilled."

2. Affirmations should focus on actions to improve our self-esteem. They should highlight our strengths and qualities that we consider important.

3. Like prayers, the most effective times for affirmations are before sleep and after waking up. Before sleeping, our subconscious mind is most receptive to affirmations, as the conscious mind is tired and less active. When done immediately upon waking up, affirmations set a positive tone for the day. We can also affirm how we want to be

during the day, further enhancing our mind-set.

4. Affirmations can be practiced throughout the day to uplift our mood and increase confidence in performing daily tasks. Depending on convenience, we can repeat affirmations every hour or before starting each task. An appropriate affirmation for the situation is sufficient and takes no more than ten seconds.

There are various ways to practice affirmations. You can say them out loud in front of a mirror, write them in a journal, or repeat them like a mantra in your mind. Written affirmations have a greater impact than oral ones. Creating credit card-sized affirmation cards to carry in your purse or placing stickers with affirmations in your room are also effective methods. Another creative idea is to use passwords for digital devices that remind you of your affirmations.

Choosing affirmations that resonate with you at the given moment is important. If you say, "I am beautiful" when you consider yourself ordinary-looking, or "I am rich" when facing financial challenges, these affirmations may feel fake and lack belief. However, inner beauty can be improved, leading to enhanced personality traits. It's worth noting that affirmations may not bring instant results, even with dedicated effort.

While affirmations may not guarantee success in achieving external factors beyond our control, they work wonderfully well for personal improvement when practiced correctly and consistently. Louise Stapely [25] recommends a step-by-step approach for refining affirmations to align with an individual's growth journey. Affirmations should make us feel differently about areas of concern, allowing us to think, believe, and act more positively and productively. An example of stepwise modification of a basic affirmation is provided below:

Basic affirmation: "I achieve my goals quickly and easily."

 Modified affirmations

  - "I am capable of achieving my goals quickly and easily."

  - "I am eager to achieve my goals quickly and easily."

  - "I am ready to achieve my goals quickly and easily."

Observe the difference in these affirmations. The modified versions include emotionally charged words like "capable," "eager," and "ready." By triggering our emotions, they enhance our motivation, determination, and overall level of action-taking. The true power of affirmations lies in their transformation into our feelings, beliefs, and behaviors.

Although the standard recommendation is to use affirmations in the present tense, some variations can be used if they resonate with you. For example:

  - "I am happy."

  - "I love to be happy."

  - "I choose to be happy."

Each variant has its unique advantage. The first allows for visualizing the desired condition, regardless of the present situation. Failing to understand this crucial difference can make people feel like they are affirming something fake, leading to disbelief and ineffective results. The second variant avoids confusion by emphasizing the feeling, which appeals to logic. The third variant is interesting because it indicates a conscious choice and a sense of responsibility to act.

To help you get started, here are some examples of basic affirmations. Remember, you can modify them to suit your specific needs and preferences at any given moment:

For Self-Love
- "I love and accept myself as I am."
For Self-Esteem
- "I am a good decision-maker."
For Developing Good Qualities
Consider qualities like confidence, capability, courage, discipline, punctuality, trustworthiness, truthfulness, determination, honesty, humility, sincerity, compassion, patience, and motivation.
For Confidence
- "I am a confident person."
For Good Health and Energy
- "I am energetic and full of vitality."
For Peace and Happiness
- "I am serene, tranquil, and happy."
For Faith and God
- "I believe I can handle all situations that may arise today to the best of my ability with God's grace."
For Love and Relationships
- "I am full of love, respect, blessings, compassion, and care for others."
For Work
- "I visualize doing my best in everything I do today."
For General Improvement
- "Every day, in every way, I am getting better."
For Beliefs
- "I believe in natural abundance. I see opportunities."
Tal-Ben Shahar [1] shares a list of eight affirming messages that serve as his guide to a better life. Each morning, he spends half a minute on each message, contemplating what it means to him, imagining the desired state, and feeling what embodying those qualities is like.
For those who wish to explore affirmations more, valuable

resources are available on YouTube.

In the next chapter, we'll explore the role of gratitude in fostering a positive outlook.

• • •

CHAPTER VIII

Gratitude: A Tool for Transforming Life

"The root of joy is gratefulness ...It is not joy that makes us grateful; it is gratitude that makes us joyful. " – Brother David Steindl-Rast

The Significance of Gratitude

What we focus on in our thoughts determines what manifests in our lives. By actively acknowledging the things we are grateful for, we attract even more reasons to be grateful. Without realizing it, we often fixate on the negatives, which only contribute to our unhappiness.

We have been conditioned to believe that external circumstances dictate our happiness. However, the most profound form of gratitude stems from the mere fact that we are alive as human beings. It is an extraordinary blessing to be born into the most intelligent species on Earth.

Gratitude is a powerful form of prayer, enabling us to connect deeply with God or the Universal Power. When we express gratitude, we demonstrate trust in life itself. It is the essence of all virtues, encompassing compassion, resilience, kindness, confidence, and passion.

Happy individuals are consistently grateful for the factors that bring them happiness. Scientific studies have confirmed that consciously cultivating gratitude leads to increased happiness. By practicing gratitude, we train our minds to seek out the positive aspects of life, effectively rewiring our brains. This rewiring process creates a feedback loop, shifting our focus away from stress and negativity.

Engaging in gratitude practices holds profound significance. It prevents us from overlooking the good things surrounding us, countering the negative influences perpetuated by various media outlets that often sensationalize wars, crimes, corruption, and other negative aspects, distorting our perception of life.

One prevalent issue we face is taking the priceless gifts of nature and the contributions of others for granted. This tendency is even more pronounced with our loved ones. In happy families, gratitude and appreciation become a way of life, encompassing even the smallest gestures or accomplishments.

The Impact of Gratitude Studies

Martin Seligman, a proponent of positive psychology, encourages his students to write gratitude letters and embark on gratitude visits to express their appreciation to the people they care about. This simple exercise often profoundly affects both the writer and the recipient, strengthening their relationship. It goes beyond a mere thank-you note by capturing specific experiences, shared dreams, and other aspects of the relationship that bring joy [1].

Neuroscientist Alex Corb from UCLA [26] discovered that gratitude releases dopamine, the brain's reward chemical, evoking a desire to repeat the experience. When gratitude becomes habitual, the brain actively seeks more opportunities for reward, creating a virtuous cycle.

Extensive research has been conducted to explore the positive effects of gratitude. In a study by Emmon and McCullough [27], four groups were randomly assigned to write for three minutes before bedtime. The first group wrote about things they were grateful for, and the second group focused on daily hassles, the third group reflected on areas where they believed they outperformed others, and the last group had the freedom to write about anything. They continued this practice for six months, and their physical health, optimism, happiness, and benevolence were monitored for six months to one year. The "gratitude" group consistently demonstrated the most positive outcomes across all parameters, while the "hassles" group fared the worst.

Psychologist Robert Emmons dedicated his entire career to studying gratitude, and he identified a few elements that are integral to our well-being, such as gratitude [27]. Countless studies have confirmed that individuals who consistently practice gratitude exhibit higher levels of energy, emotional intelligence, forgiveness, and a reduced likelihood of experiencing depression, anxiety, or loneliness. Gratitude has been proven to be a significant catalyst for positive outcomes [1]. Even a few weeks of gratitude exercises can increase happiness, optimism, sociability, improved sleep, and fewer headaches [1].

For a group of college students plagued by worries and racing thoughts, writing down what they were grateful for before bed resulted in reduced rumination and improved sleep quality [1].

Practicing Gratitude: Things to Be Grateful for

Let us take every opportunity to express gratitude, appreciation, and admiration [28]. Here are a few suggestions to consider upon waking up:

- God, the Universe, Earth, nature, plants, animals, people
- Our bodies, health, and the privilege of work or studies
- Money, relationships, friends, and the comfort of our

homes
- Material possessions such as cars, phones, and other goods

Before sleeping, let us reflect on three positive occurrences during the day. Explore the reasons behind them and genuinely say "Thank You." If it proves challenging to identify something from the current day, we can look back on previous days. Remember, these moments need not be grand gestures but anything that brings a smile to our faces. Express gratitude to three individuals before sleeping. It can include relatives, friends, or colleagues who have positively impacted your life.

Gratitude should extend to our resources and money, no matter how meager they may be [28]. Complaining about scarcity only perpetuates more scarcity. During times of financial constraint, let us remember periods when we had more and express gratitude for those times. Rather than harboring jealousy toward the wealthy, let us admire their hard work and pray for the prosperity of those less fortunate. Whenever we receive a bill, let us thank God for providing the means to settle it.

Let us be grateful for our good health, appreciating every cell in our bodies for its remarkable function. Express gratitude for being alive each morning upon waking up and for the well-being of our family members. During illness, let us recall times when we were in excellent health and express gratitude for those moments. Additionally, let us proactively thank God for restoring good health and extending these prayers to our loved ones. Instead of fixating on sickness, let us focus on good health.

Even if our current situation or job opportunity falls short of our expectations, let us express gratitude for the opportunity itself. This mindset paves the way for attracting better prospects in the future.

Express gratitude daily for the air we breathe, the water we drink, and other natural resources that sustain us. Similarly, let us be thankful for our food, regardless of its modesty.

Identify a few challenging relationships that could benefit from improvement. In these instances, find at least one positive aspect to appreciate and be grateful for. Blame, anger, and hatred harm relationships, while gratitude fosters healing.

When expressing gratitude, immerse yourself in the meaning of each item and genuinely experience the associated emotions. Sharing gratitude can significantly enhance relationships.

During a walk, say "Thank you for the next hundred steps" with each stride, allowing it to uplift your mood [28].

Place your right hand on your heart, close your eyes, and say, "Thank you." This practice boosts both your immune system and your mood. Express gratitude to every organ and cell in your body for their efficient function throughout the years.

Practice gratitude for upcoming events such as interviews, exams, or meetings, envisioning successful outcomes.

The environment around us provides numerous cues for gratitude. When we encounter a hospital or an ambulance, we express gratitude for our good health. When we see a bank or an ATM, let us be grateful for the financial resources we possess. When encountering someone less fortunate, offer prayers for their well-being and express gratitude for our job or business [28].

When you face a mirror, smile at your reflection and express gratitude for your identity. Remember, the world's appearance changes according to our mood, and true magic and beauty reside within. By altering our mindset, we can transform the world around us.

In the next chapter, we will explore the formation of habits.

• • •

CHAPTER IX

The Science and Benefits of Habits

"Watch your thoughts, they become your words; watch your words, they become your actions; watch your actions, they become your habits; watch your habits, they become your character; watch your character, it becomes your destiny." - *Lao Tzu.*

Understanding Habits

Without even realizing it, we often find ourselves bound by our habits. Our brains are wired to create habits for energy conservation and efficient action. However, many habits are formed unconsciously and can harm our overall happiness. To improve our lives, we must first become aware of our habits in all areas and then gradually challenge ourselves to break free from the negative ones and replace them with positive ones.

When we encounter a new situation, our brains are highly active, processing a lot of information to find a solution. However, once a situation repeats, the brain recognizes it and knows the answer, resulting in reduced activity and preserved energy. This is how habits are formed, providing reliable solutions to recurring problems.

We can't just say "I am happy" or "I love to be happy" because it quickly wears off. Although we can choose happiness even when life is challenging, that choice must be accompanied by conscious, positive habit changes to see any benefit.

Success is a Process

Success is not an isolated event but a result of consistent small disciplines that lead us to develop habitual patterns of success. These patterns eventually become ingrained in us and no longer require constant willpower or effort [15]. Understanding what truly matters to us serves as motivation for our actions. However, even with this knowledge, our willpower diminishes over time with use. Therefore, it's important to replenish and use it judiciously. As mentioned earlier, habits are particularly effective for repetitive tasks, allowing us to conserve energy. Willpower plays a crucial role during the initial phase of habit formation, where we must keep the steps small to avoid willpower fatigue and ensure success.

Discovering Our Habits

Gaining insight into our habits requires patience and visualization of our daily repetitive activities. By keeping a journal and noting down our habits while assessing whether they are good or bad, we can lay the foundation for significant improvement in our lives. It is best to focus on one activity at a time, observing how we engage in it. This process of self-awareness sets the stage for maximum personal growth.

Developing New Habits

Four steps are involved in habit formation [29]: Cue, Craving, Activity, and Reward. The cue serves as a trigger that reminds us of the craving, which is our desire. This prompts us to engage in an activity that produces a satisfying reward. Visual cues have a particularly strong influence on habit formation. While cultivating a new habit, it is important to create obvious cues that remind us to act. Understanding the benefits of the new habit and planning for it in advance, specifying what, how much, when, and where, significantly enhances the chances of success. Formulating implementation intentions, such as "When X happens, I will do Y," is a crucial aspect of habit formation [29].

For making a habit stick, it's helpful to make it addictive by triggering the release of dopamine, a happiness chemical in the brain. Interestingly, even anticipating the reward releases dopamine and motivates action. Psychologists have found that the anticipation of a vacation or a festival can be more enjoyable than the experience. We can use this knowledge to our advantage and repeat good behaviors.

Sustaining Good Habits

Joining a like-minded group can greatly assist in sustaining good habits. As the saying goes, "A lone wolf dies, a pack survives." We tend to imitate the habits of those closest to us, the larger groups we belong to, and the most influential individuals around us. By carefully selecting the groups we associate with, we can avoid bad habits and improve our good ones. Finding a group that embodies the culture and habits we aspire to have can be highly beneficial.

We can develop a short happiness routine, like how athletes use warm-up routines to prepare themselves physically and mentally before a competition. This routine may involve taking three deep breaths, smiling, and reciting a positive affirmation before undertaking any important task. It can be done anywhere, anytime, improving our mood, even in stressful or sad situations.

Focus on Consistency, Not Perfection

The frequency of performing an activity is more important than executing it perfectly. Voltaire once said, "The best is the enemy of good." Spending excessive time crafting an optimal plan is unnecessary. Setting suboptimal goals and acting is what truly matters. By keeping expectations low enough to make starting and maintaining the habit easy, we can overcome the brain's inclination for laziness and convenience. For example, doing just one push-up, reading, or writing one paragraph is incredibly manageable. The brain doesn't object to such small steps; interestingly, this approach often leads to doing more than we initially intended.

The initial effort required for a new habit should not exceed two minutes. This might mean simply laying out a yoga mat, opening a book, accessing study notes, meditating for one minute, or putting on running shoes for a short jog. The crucial mastery habit is showing up for the activity. Only by showing up can we improve. To ensure success in habit development, doing the minimum required daily and avoiding consecutive days without practicing the habit is important.

Overcoming Bad Habits

When removing bad habits, it's crucial to remember that we are not helpless victims; we have a choice and can make positive changes. One effective strategy is to make the habit more difficult to sustain. For instance, if distractions from our phones or laptops hinder our productivity, we can switch them off and keep them in a cupboard a few meters away.

Tracking Progress and Immediate Rewards

Maintaining a daily record of our progress in habits is an excellent practice. It allows us to visualize our efforts and provides self-motivation. Benjamin Franklin famously used a daily diary to monitor his progress in improving his thirteen chosen virtues [7].

To make a habit stick, providing us with immediate rewards is helpful. For example, while the long-term reward of regular exercise may be improved health, the immediate rewards can be the feeling of well-being after a workout or the enjoyment of spending time with friends at the gym. During our morning walks, we can appreciate the fresh air, the scents of flowers, and the melody of birds singing. These immediate rewards contribute to our happiness, making us less concerned about long-term benefits.

The Power of Decisive Moments

Throughout the day, there are crucial moments where our choices significantly impact our lives. For instance, when the morning alarm rings, choosing to press the snooze or off button and remain in bed reinforces indiscipline. On the other hand, even if we don't feel like it, choosing to wake up and start the day reinforces our disciplined personal identity. Attending the day's first lecture on time is another example of a decisive habit. Adopting habits such as setting regular sleep hours, engaging in prayer, expressing gratitude, practicing affirmations before sleep and upon waking, and doing hourly mindfulness exercises and prayer can significantly improve our lives.

Gradual Changes for Lasting Results

Introducing one or two habits at a time and ensuring they become ingrained before introducing new ones is a wise approach. Incremental changes are more likely to succeed, as small successes tend to build upon themselves. Conversely, ambitious changes often lead to failure.

It's important to note that the effects of a habit become visible only after a threshold has been reached, which typically takes about three to four weeks of consistent activity. Just like a stonecutter who strikes a stone a hundred times without visible progress, it only takes one more blow to crack it. The same principle applies to habits—perseverance is key.

However, it's important to remember that any behavior change must align with our sense of self. We must cultivate a new identity that aligns with our desired goals to adopt new habits successfully. Pride in this new identity provides added motivation to stick to our habits. Our actions reflect the person we believe to be, so addressing identity conflicts becomes crucial to habit formation. If we dislike discipline, for instance, it will be challenging to develop regular exercise or study habits.

Continual self-improvement requires constant reflection and adjustment of our beliefs and identity. By repeating a behavior consistently, we reinforce our chosen identity. The frequency and intensity of our actions play a significant role in shaping our habits. For specific purposes and goals, later chapters will delve into the details of forming good habits.

The upcoming chapter will integrate the concepts discussed thus far into a comprehensive "Happiness Practice." By implementing these strategies, college students can create positive habits that lead to lasting success and happiness in their academic and personal lives.

• • •

CHAPTER X

Happiness Practice: A Daily Guide

"Don't wait to strike till the iron is hot; but make it hot by striking." - William Butler Yeats.

The Importance of Happiness Practice

We must practice improving in any area of life, such as studies, games, business, fitness, or music. Similarly, we need to practice happiness to become skilled at being happy. It's like playing a role in a play or a movie—we want to give our best and appear natural in every situation. Therefore, we should think and behave as a happy people would. Since we aspire to lifelong happiness, we must practice it throughout our lives.

Even if we have brushed our teeth for decades, we will get cavities if we stop. The same is true for happiness. Because if we don't practice it, our brain defaults to scanning for threats.

"Optimism is a daily spiritual practice, and when we do it, we can transform this world." Shawn Achor

We unknowingly practice unhappiness due to constant exposure to negative news, discussions, and comparisons in the media, society, family, and colleagues. These factors contribute to our unconscious negativity.

Jim Loehr and Tony Schwartz assert that the real obstacle to high performance is not stress but rather the lack of disciplined, intermittent recovery. Our lives consist of cycles of energy depletion and replenishment, both physically, emotionally, and spiritually. Listening to music we enjoy, spending time with loved ones, or taking vacations helps recharge our emotional and spiritual batteries. This chapter will explore how happiness practice accomplishes the same purpose.

Creating a Positive Day

We have the power to shape our days according to our expectations. By bringing the right emotions to each situation, we can make the most of our days and infuse them with cheerfulness. Emotions are contagious and can influence the moods of those around us.

According to Tal-Ben Shahar [1], the most significant increase in well-being he experienced did not result from a major life transformation. Instead, it was due to incorporating what he calls "happiness boosters"—small activities that elevate his mood. These mini-breaks provide the fuel he needs to maintain energy and zest. Rather than waiting until his energy levels are dangerously depleted, Tal-Ben Shahar regularly incorporated moments of instant gratification into his life. These bursts of joy make him feel better in the moment and generate enthusiasm and energy that enhance productivity, creativity, and overall happiness.

This chapter focuses on happiness practice in our non-academic activities, extending its benefits to academic pursuits. Part II of this book will thoroughly discuss happiness practice in academic activities.

Understanding Happiness Practice

In the previous chapters, we explored the factors that contribute to happiness. Now, we will delve into integrating these elements into our daily routines. Any activity we want to engage in regularly must become a habit to minimize effort. First and foremost, we must cultivate the habit of believing we can be happy and successful through affirmations. This foundational habit facilitates the development of all other happiness habits.

Love, peace, and happiness are interconnected qualities. Therefore, we can practice any of these to enhance our happiness. While achieving success without self-love is possible, true happiness requires a reasonable degree of self-love. Thus, it is crucial to practice self-love as frequently as possible.

We should implement the strategies discussed earlier from the moment we wake up until we go to sleep. We can reduce negativity and consciously embrace positivity by incorporating love, positive thinking, meditation, prayers, affirmations, and gratitude. Happiness practice is not a one-time or one-day endeavor; it should become a continuous way of living.

One of the most significant actions we can take is to cultivate a new "Happy" identity by affirming to ourselves multiple times a day, "I am a happy person" or "I love being happy." We should take pride in this new identity, even if we don't share it with others. Self-talk plays a vital role in this process.

Time Management

Every happy and successful person is skilled in time management. A detailed chapter on this topic is in Part II of this book. When we schedule all our activities, including classes, studies, recreation, social relationships, rest, and physical and mental fitness, we experience a sense of relaxation. It is crucial to include even the smallest tasks in our timetable. Periodic performance reviews are integral to effective time management as they provide valuable feedback for improvement. By addressing uncertainties and contingencies through proper planning, we can reduce stress and experience greater peace. Balance is key in time management.

Self-Awareness

As explained in Chapter 4, we must understand what triggers our emotions and affects our body and mind. This knowledge enables us to become better individuals, find balance, and improve our relationships.

Additionally, we should check our mood throughout the day. Amidst a hectic work schedule, it can be challenging to remember this. However, we can make it an intelligent habit by checking our mood during breaks, such as when using the washroom or before consuming food or beverages. When we realize we are not in a good mood, we can employ the measures discussed later in the book.

Establishing a Shut-down Routine

The period before sleep is crucial for setting the tone for a peaceful sleep and an efficient, joyful next day. To ensure this, we must engage in the following activities according to our prearranged timetable. If we are pressed for time on some days, we can allocate a minimum amount of time to each activity rather than skipping them entirely.

Approximately 15-30 minutes before sleep, we should stop all other work and switch digital devices off. This allows us to avoid stimulating content on TV or other devices that could hinder peaceful sleep.

Reading a few pages, at least one, from inspirational books, articles, or biographies is highly recommended. Dedicating at least 30 minutes to reading on weekends and holidays is desirable. Keeping the selected material near our bed for easy access is a practical idea.

Daily journaling is one of the most important practices before going to sleep. It enables us to bring our deeper thoughts and concerns into focus, aiding in self-reflection and improvement. Negative experiences can linger in our memory throughout the day, making it essential to flush them out before sleep to achieve peace.

Expressing gratitude in our journal for at least one thing in life and the reason behind it is crucial. To cover a wide range of things, we should change the focus of our gratitude each day, encompassing various aspects of our lives. We may spend more time doing this activity on weekends or holidays.

Expressing admiration and appreciation for the good things done by others brings us happiness and reveals our positive qualities.

Following the exercises discussed in Chapter 2, we can practice self-love affirmations in front of a mirror for optimal results. Additionally, we should express love for our mind and body.

Reflecting on how we spent the previous day, we can recall three things that brought us happiness. These moments can be from any area of life that brings a smile to our faces. If we have achieved something we're proud of, we can record it in our "Diary of Excellence."

Forgiving those who may have hurt us during the day is important, but seeking forgiveness from those we have hurt is even more crucial. If we're uncomfortable discussing this with others, we can do it privately in our minds. It is equally important to forgive ourselves for any wrongs we may have committed.

Engaging in conversation with God or a Higher Power, sharing our joys and frustrations as we would with a loving parent, is a beneficial practice. As described in earlier chapters, this can be followed by a few minutes of mindful deep breathing, offering prayers, and reciting affirmations. We can even seek guidance and assistance in handling specific problems or difficult individuals. Before sleep, we should express our fears, anger, hatred, and jealousy, entrusting all our worries to God. Lastly, let us pray for a peaceful sleep and wake up cheerful and confident, remembering that our waking thoughts influence our day.

As discussed in Chapter 2, adhering to good sleep hygiene is crucial for optimal energy and mood management.

Establishing a Start-Up Routine

Starting the day with a positive mindset is essential. During this time, we should avoid using digital devices. Before getting out of bed, let us express gratitude for the good things in our lives. We can also engage in prayers, as discussed in Chapter 6, and make appropriate affirmations according to Chapter 7. Rushing out of bed should be avoided. Our bodies have rested for seven hours, so we must gradually ease into the day. When we finally get up, let us fold the comforter and make the bed neatly. This small act of discipline sets a positive tone and creates momentum for accomplishing more throughout the day, instantly uplifting our mood.

Since long hours of sleep cause dehydration, we must hydrate ourselves by drinking at least one glass of lukewarm water upon waking up. We can mindfully prepare coffee or tea and savor each sip while remaining relaxed. Ideally, we can enjoy our beverage on the balcony or in open spaces, observing the morning scene outside. If the weather is unfavorable, we can still open the curtains or shades and take in the surroundings. During these moments, we should practice mindfulness, savoring the outdoors, the taste of our drink, and internal peace and joy. This deliberate ten to fifteen minutes of relaxation revitalizes us for the day ahead.

Looking Smart and Creating a Positive Environment

It is important to feel and look attractive not only for others but also for us. Wearing clean, well-ironed clothes and comfortable shoes enhances our sense of well-being. This positive feeling has a ripple effect on our actions and thoughts throughout the day. I remember asking my late father, who was in his 90s, why he shaved and applied perfume daily when his social engagement was negligible. He told me that he did not do it for others but because it made him feel good.

Our personal space, particularly our room, plays a significant role in our well-being. It should be a place where we feel good and relaxed. Keeping our room clean, making the bed neatly, and maintaining a tidy study table contribute to a positive atmosphere. Everything in the room should have its designated place, and we should develop a habit of ensuring it remains organized. Placing photographs of loved ones and representations of our chosen deity on our working table can uplift our mood. Adding inspiring posters and quotes on the walls or desktop background can also positively impact us. Fresh flowers and the aroma of incense can create a pleasant ambiance.

Meditation

Meditation is a vital activity for cultivating inner peace and joy. It provides much-needed rest for our busy minds and connects us to our inner consciousness, which grants us strength and wisdom to face life's challenges. The process of meditation has already been described in Chapter 4.

We can start with three minutes of meditation and gradually increase the duration as our desire grows.

Mindfulness Meditation

As explained in Chapter 4, practicing mindfulness throughout the day helps us maintain a meditative state in all our activities. It acts as an oasis of peace amidst the desert of daily life, preventing compulsive thinking.

Special Journaling Exercise

Devoting 15-20 minutes to writing about hardships or difficult experiences in a journal can alleviate stress. Afterward, we can discard or delete the entry. On the other hand, writing about positive experiences for 20 minutes a day, three times a week, significantly boosts happiness. Moreover, the effects of this exercise last longer, even if we eventually stop doing it.

Hourly and Need-Based Mind Control

Every hour, let us pause and take a few deep, mindful breaths. During this time, we can offer prayers and make one or two affirmations for peace, happiness, and strength. Affirming self-love is a periodic mood booster, relieving stress and preventing its accumulation. This entire process takes less than a minute. Setting hourly alarms can remind us to engage in these practices. Additionally, we can employ the same techniques whenever we detect negativity and stress. Since these activities go unnoticed by others, we can practice them anywhere, anytime, even during the busiest and most stressful periods.

Let us engage in the following exercise whenever we have free moments to inject instant joy. Silently wishing happiness for a few known or unknown individuals can generate tremendous goodwill with minimal effort. Similarly, silently wishing for alleviating suffering for those we know are going through difficult times is a powerful act. This practice can be done anytime, anywhere. Taking 3 to 4 deep breaths, preferably with eyes closed, can help us enter an upward spiral of calm, even in the most stressful situations, preventing a downward spiral caused by stress.

Stress Busters

We can discover our most effective stress busters based

on personal preferences. These activities can be utilized when we feel stressed or to prevent stress from building up. Some well-known stress busters include listening to soothing music and happy songs, surrounding us with fresh flowers, engaging in aerobic exercise, viewing pictures or videos of loved ones, admiring the beautiful scenery, reading inspiring quotes, enjoying humor and jokes, and even taking short ten-minute naps, which can be remarkably energizing. Taking mindful walks in green areas or lawns is another effective stress-reducing practice. We can incorporate this into our daily routine, even if it's only for a short period when stress arises. Spending a few hours in a nearby park on weekends can be a rejuvenating experience. Planning trips with friends during summer or winter vacations significantly reduces stress.

Looking forward to something interesting also helps alleviate stress. Anticipating future rewards, such as scheduling a favorite movie or planning a vacation or dinner with friends, can increase endorphin levels by 27%. Putting these events on a calendar and anticipating them activates the pleasure center in our brains.

Exercise releases endorphins, which induce pleasure. It boosts mood, enhances work performance, increases motivation, and reduces stress and anxiety. It is important to incorporate these stress busters into our timetable whenever possible.

Building Relationships

The easiest way to experience happiness is by surrounding ourselves with positive and happy friends or family members. Spending free time with them infects us with their positivity and happiness.

When we spend time with friends or family, let us prioritize improving our relationships by doing something that brings them joy. Instead of expecting things from others, let us focus on giving within our comfort level. Giving doesn't always require money; it can be as simple as offering prayers, sharing a warm smile, giving a heartfelt compliment or appreciation, and expressing gratitude. These acts serve as deposits in our emotional bank, providing support during difficult times. The happiness derived from these acts is invaluable.

To maintain harmony with others, we must prioritize good behavior and actions. Love, respect, and the well-being of others should always be at the forefront of our minds. It is beneficial to help and empower others to the best of our abilities. When dealing with others, adopting a "win-win" approach is advisable.

"I have learned that people will forget what you said, people will forget what you did, but people will never forget how you made them feel." - Maya Angelou.

Maintaining connections with positive family members is essential. Sharing positive and negative experiences with them establishes a support system during challenging times.

It is crucial to avoid toxic people who disempower and demotivate us. If it is impossible to avoid them completely, we should minimize interactions with them as much as possible. Furthermore, engaging in arguments with such individuals should be avoided.

Practicing Good Qualities

As discussed in Chapter 1, continuous improvement in cultivating positive qualities forms the foundation for sustainable happiness and success in both professional and personal life. Identifying the qualities, we want to improve and monitoring our progress daily is important. Punctuality, trustworthiness, truthfulness, and ethical behavior are some of the qualities we can focus on.

Each of us possesses a unique skill or character virtue. Actively exercising and honing these abilities provides a significant happiness boost.

Laugh and Smile

Sometimes your joy is the source of your smile, but sometimes your smile can be the source of your joy." - Thich Nhat Hanh.

Research on the "facial feedback hypothesis" conducted by psychologists indicates that facial expressions can influence mood. Simply smiling can induce a more positive feeling. We can improve our mood at any given moment by intentionally smiling or laughing. This can be achieved by thinking of something we love, recalling a funny story or situation, or even faking a smile until the emotion becomes genuine.

To overcome stage fright, Tal-Ben Shahar used to wear a genuine smile before going on stage. It instantly uplifted his mood and created a positive connection with the audience. Similarly, I used to make eye contact with a few students and offer a smiling face when entering the classroom, silently praying for their well-being.

A hearty laugh at least three times a day and smiling at every opportunity (at least five times a day) are essential practices. Keeping track of how often we engage in these activities can help maintain a joyful disposition.

Handling Worries

Worries consume a significant amount of time and energy. Being in a negative mood reduces our work efficiency and negatively impacts our relationships.

As discussed in Chapter 3, when worries overwhelm us, we can assure our minds that we will allocate a specific time slot or day to address them seriously. Another approach is to write down our worries and place them in "God's

Worry Basket" before going to sleep, seeking guidance on tackling them. Occasionally, practicing a "Worry Fast" for a short period and gradually extending it weakens the habit of worrying.

Acceptance

As explained in Chapter 3, it is important to accept situations and individuals, including their behaviors, with love. We should strive to improve whatever aspects we can, as guided by the serenity prayer. Accepting our weaknesses, failures, and fluctuating moods without harboring negativity or resentment is essential. Observing our emotions from a third-person perspective becomes easier to manage.

Positive Self-talk and Visualization

Instead of defaulting to harmful habits of recalling past hurts and failures, we should consciously recollect positive experiences from our past using our Diary of Excellence. Similarly, when contemplating the future, we should visualize ourselves lovingly doing our best and enjoying each moment. Consciously engaging with the happy past and future improves our mood and instills confidence. Detailed visualization of our desired outcomes is more effective than merely thinking about them. Top performers in various fields utilize this technique. If visualization proves challenging, imagining our emotions when achieving our goals can also be effective.

Importance of Body Postures

Our body postures communicate our level of confidence and energy. Slumped shoulders, dragging feet, and a downward gaze convey a lack of confidence. Conversely, walking with a strong stride and open, relaxed shoulders sends a positive message to us and others. Sitting up straight actually boosts our motivation and increases our energy. Engaging in firm handshakes promotes assertiveness. We should take pride in adopting powerful postures.

Joyful Action

Approaching our professional and personal endeavors with love is essential, regardless of the nature of the task, whether it be mundane or significant. Conditioning our minds through affirmations such as "I love doing..." or "I am happy doing..." helps foster this attitude. Bringing mindfulness and curiosity to everything we do is also beneficial.

Noticing Minor and Routine Moments of Joy

Every day, we experience many fleeting moments of joy that often go unnoticed because we take them for granted. These include the first bite of food when hungry, the first sip of water when thirsty, the sensation of warm water droplets during a shower in winter, or the relief of cool air inside an air-conditioned room or car after exposure to hot weather. We need to train our minds to notice and appreciate these moments. When we wake up in the morning, let us smile with gratitude for being alive and healthy. Training ourselves to value life and health, which are fundamental, is important. Often, we take these blessings for granted. What we consistently focus on grows, making this simple happiness practice essential.

Effective Use of Free Time

Indulging in passive leisure during our free time may provide temporary rest, but it does not necessarily improve our mood and energy. Despite the effort involved, engaging in hobbies or other activities that challenge us mentally or physically and leaves us feeling refreshed. It is important to have a support system of individuals who care about our well-being and with whom we can share our happiness practice plans. Regularly updating them on our progress holds us accountable and allows them to complement and motivate us during successful and challenging moments.

Here is a summary of happiness practices that can be incorporated into daily life. Beginners can start with the practices that resonate with them, but engaging in most of them in the long run is beneficial. Some practices can be done for a minimum duration instead of focusing on a few for an extended period while neglecting others.

1. Affirmation about belief in becoming happy: Repeat in the evening and morning - 10 seconds
2. Self-love affirmations: Repeat at least one affirmation in the evening, morning, and when in front of the mirror - 10 seconds
3. Other affirmations: Repeat at least one affirmation as needed - 10-20 seconds
4. Prayers: Say at least one prayer in the evening, morning, and whenever needed - 10-30 seconds
5. Meditation: Practice meditation in the evening or morning - 2-10 minutes
6. Mindfulness: Practice mindfulness while walking or listening, integrating it into daily activities without requiring extra time
7. Mindful deep breaths: Take a minimum of three deep breaths hourly or at any time - 15-30 seconds
8. Gratitude: Express gratitude before sleep and in the morning - 2-3 minutes
9. Recollect good things in the day: Before sleep, recall at least one positive experience from the day - 2-3 minutes
10. Reading inspiring material: Read at least one page of inspiring content in the evening - 3-5 minutes

11. Journaling thoughts: Spend 3-5 minutes in the evening to write down thoughts and reflections
12. Smile: Aim to smile at least ten times throughout the day - No extra time is needed
13. Laughs: Find moments to laugh at least five times per day - No extra time is needed
14. Exercise: Schedule suitable aerobic exercise for 1-30 minutes - as per schedule
15. Stress busters: Allocate scheduled time for stress-relieving activities lasting 3-10 minutes
16. Relationships: Dedicate scheduled time for phone calls or personal meetings with loved ones - as per schedule

• • •

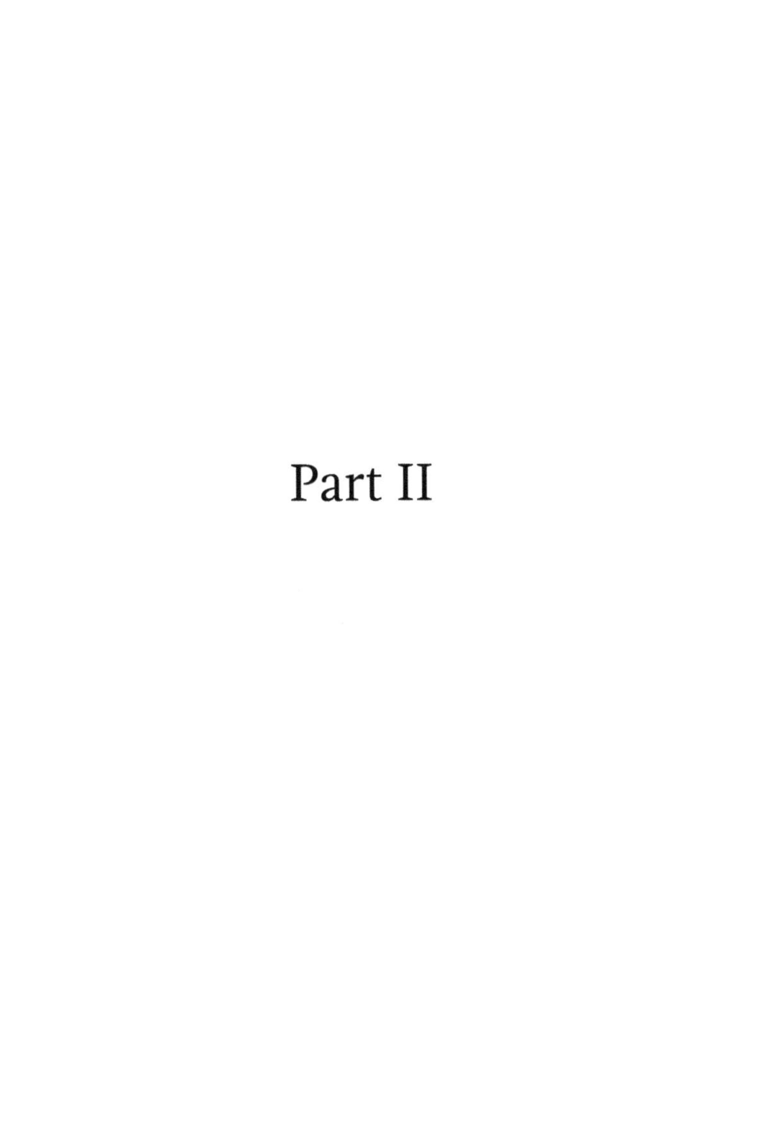

Part II

CHAPTER XI

The Art of Joyful Learning

"Be all you can be, whatever that is for you. Reach for your best. Finish strong. It means consistent focusing and doing your absolute best at every moment, from start to finish. No whining. No complaining. No excuses." Seattle Seahawks Motto

Part II of the book begins by exploring the mindset and approach needed for enjoying your academics. It then delves into the significance of effective time management for achieving both success and happiness. We will also cover strategies for maximizing the benefits of lectures, study sessions, and exam preparation. You'll find a thorough discussion of all facets of research. Additionally, we will delve into the valuable lessons learned from failures through real-life case studies. Finally, we will offer practical tips to help you prepare for a bright future after completing your current study program.

Developing Qualities for Success

Student life encompasses more than just studying and obtaining degrees. It is also about personal growth and development, which is essential for success in life. Alongside academics, it's crucial to cultivate good relationships, strengthen our bodies and minds, and develop important qualities. To be both happy and successful, we must adopt the identity of a happy student. This means embodying qualities such as punctuality, sincerity, hard work, and ethical consciousness. Unfortunately, society has often led us to believe that working less, resorting to unfair means, sacrificing sleep for fun, and pretending to be happy even when we are not desirable traits.

Consider if you were an employer, would you hire a highly intelligent individual lacking these qualities or someone slightly less intelligent but possessing them? Similarly, when looking for.a life partner, would you prefer someone lacking fidelity and trust or someone who possesses these qualities? If we acknowledge what is valued universally, why do we think society will exempt us from those values? Therefore, we must take pride in cultivating these qualities through repeated affirmations.

Tal-Ben Shahar suggests a valuable self-help exercise: *"One of the most useful self-help exercises that I carry out involves reading a list of characteristics that, for me, capture the way I want to think about myself and the way I want to be"* [1].

We all Have Potential; Our Sacred Duty is to Realize it:

Following are some of the observations in this regard by Angela Duckworth in her book 'Grit' [23].

The Harvard admissions in charge for 40 years says: *"My sense is that most people are born with tremendous potential. The real question is whether they are encouraged to employ their good old fashioned hard work and their grit to maximum. In the end, those are the people who seem to be most successful."*

Best school students were distinguished more by their work ethic than by their intelligence.

A famous quote from Darwin: *"Excepting fools, men did not differ much in intellect, only in zeal and hard work."* He said about himself: *"I think I am superior to the common man in noticing things which easily escape attention, and in observing them carefully."*

A quote from the famous author William James: *"Compared with what we ought to be, we are only half awake. Our fires are*

damped; our drafts are checked. We are making use of only a small part of our possible mental and physical resources."
He further observed: *"The human individual lives usually far within his limits; he possesses powers of various sorts which he habitually fails to use. He energises below his maximum, and he behaves below his optimum."*
Dan Chambliss, a sociologist, observed from a study: *"Superlative performance is really a confluence of dozens of small skills or activities, each one learned or stumbled upon, which have been carefully drilled into habit and then are fitted together in a synthesized whole. There is nothing extraordinary or superhuman in any one of these actions; only the fact that they are done consistently and correctly, and all together, produce excellence."*
The important thing to remember is that greatness is doable. It involves many individual feats, and each of them is doable. High-level performance is, in fact, an accretion of mundane acts.
If we overemphasize talent, we underemphasize efforts.
Talent x effort = skill, Skill x effort = achievement
The effort builds skill, and it also makes the latter productive.
Someone twice as talented but half as hardworking as another person might reach the same skill level but still produce dramatically less over time. It is because as people who strive to improve their skills also employ the skills to produce more.
Both genes and experience influence every human trait. It applies to honesty, generosity, and IQ. Talents are not entirely genetic. The rate at which we develop any skill is also, crucially, a function of experience.
James Irving, the famous author, rewrote drafts of his novels. Since reading and writing didn't come easily, he

learned that to do anything really well, you have to overextend yourself. He said, *"I have confidence in my stamina to go over something again and again, no matter how difficult it is."*

Will Smith, the famous actor, observed: *"I have never really viewed myself as particularly talented. Where I excel is ridiculous, sickening work ethic."*

An American moviemaker and actor, Woody Allen, said: *"Eighty percent of success in life is showing up."*

Many of us start something new, full of excitement and good intentions, and then give up permanently when we encounter the first real obstacle.

Many people advise that you should do what you are passionate about. However, passion is not obsession or infatuation. It is a commitment of a different kind. Rather than intensity, it is consistency over time. Passion can develop over many years. It may not be a passive discovery process but an active construction. We can create it.

Even in the development of interest in any field, there is practicing, studying, and learning to be done. It requires time, energy, and sacrifice.

The famous author John Irving said: *"To do everything very well, you have to overextend yourself. In doing something over and over again, something that was never natural becomes almost second nature. The capacity to do work diligently doesn't come overnight."*

Atul Gawande, the famous US surgeon, shared the following secret of his success: *"Becoming a great surgeon requires practicing one difficult thing day and night for years on end."*

The gritty student affirms [23], *"I embrace the challenge of tougher courses, and I am going to apply all the grit I have to improving myself and making myself better, even if means graduating with a GPA less than what I would have earned if I had taken easier courses."*

Envisioning Your Future Early

Resolve to 'Be early.' Do it for almost everything [23].

Many students start pondering about their career choices when they're in their final year. However, initiating this process right from your first year is crucial due to its numerous advantages. By beginning early, you gain access to valuable insights from seniors. This approach also enhances your focus and prevents you from making the mistakes that uninformed students often fall into. The head start you get compared to your peers instills a greater sense of control over your situation. This heightened sense of security, in turn, positively impacts your academic performance. You can delve into the details of how to get started in the 18th chapter.

The following real-life story tells the harm done by the taking-it-easy philosophy.

A Student Who Wept at a Farewell Party

One dual degree student attended a celebration and farewell party with a few final-year B. Tech pass-out students. They had all got jobs. Suddenly, one student started weeping, to the astonishment of everyone. After a while, he revealed his anguish by saying he had wasted his four years at I.I.T. Delhi. His other friends at the party also reflected and realized that it was indeed true for all of them. This was because although they all got jobs, those were very average, and they all knew they had the talent to do much better if they had not wasted time during their stay in the institute.

Dream Big

When envisioning your future, it is beneficial to dream big, regardless of your current academic and financial status.

Instead of solely focusing on securing a job, aspiring to create jobs for others, develop innovative products, or contribute meaningfully to society. Think about uplifting your families, the organizations that may employ you, your communities, and your nation. Ambitious dreams generate enthusiasm; it doesn't matter how many dreams come to fruition. The process of pursuing them brings you happiness. Once you embrace this thinking, you'll be inclined to continue it throughout your life.

Why and How to Study?

Of all the subjects you study in school and college, only a small fraction is typically directly applicable to your professional life. However, understanding why you should approach learning joyfully and how to learn effectively is immensely valuable throughout your life. The most vital skill you acquire through education is the ability to learn how to learn. Once you recognize this, your focus shifts from grades and subject matter to cultivating this essential skill. Success in our professional lives hinges on our ongoing capacity to learn new things and apply that knowledge to tackle challenges.

To achieve happiness and success in the external world, you need integrated and robust work practices to navigate unknown challenges in an uncertain environment. As we will explore in later chapters, you must view attending classes, studying, and taking exams as interconnected efforts. In addition to these work practices, you need intensity, consistent effort, grit, and determination.

Clarity of Purpose

Your purpose depends on your philosophy of life.

Your Purpose in Life: Always do your best willingly and joyfully.

Your Purpose in College Life: Learning how best to learn.

Acquiring the best life skills and academic knowledge.

A clear, well-defined philosophy gives you guidelines and boundaries that keep you on track.

Engage in the following dialogue with yourself every day: "My studies here are an investment in a brighter future. I am fully committed and determined to give my best effort and extract the most from my teachers and resources."

Developing the Right Attitude

Apply the serenity principle to your studies. Since you chose to enroll in these courses, you will inevitably face exams, viva, reports, tutorials, and assignments. The most efficient way to approach these tasks is to shed all negativity surrounding them, such as labeling a course as boring, useless, or having a bad teacher, poor evaluation, or overwhelming workload. You must carefully assess what can be changed and what cannot. For instance, you may rarely consider leaving your current college or program. If you genuinely despise what you do, consult wise family members or well-wishers. After that, if you believe starting fresh in a different program would be better, then pursuing that path would help instead of carrying the burden indefinitely. Otherwise, you must learn to love what you do, including courses. Sulking or fretting should be avoided.

Shawn Achor [2] observed how students' attitudes affected their performance at Harvard: *"Many of my students saw Harvard as a privilege; others focused only on workload, competition, and stress. They fretted incessantly about the future, even though they were earning a degree that opened more doors. They felt overwhelmed by every small setback instead of being energized by the possibilities in front of them. These students were susceptible to stress and depression, and their grades and academic performance suffered the most. On the other hand, the students who saw it as a privilege seemed to shine even brighter."*

You can create positive change in your lives through empowering beliefs. Belief is a stronger predictor of performance than the actual level of skill. Consider a study on Asian women's math test performance that explored the impact of positive and negative beliefs. In the first instance, no specific beliefs were mentioned. In the second instance, they were told that women are weak in math. In the third instance, they were informed that Asians are good at math. The results showed that the third test yielded the best results, while the second test produced the worst.

Some students believe they cannot learn subjects like math, and others commonly perceived as difficult. However, such beliefs are unfounded and irrational. Success is possible only when you perceive yourself as capable. This belief can be developed through prayers, affirmations, and small steps. Moreover, it's more important to believe in your ability to improve rather than just believing in your current abilities.

If you develop a habit of skipping classes or arriving late, you are sowing the seeds of your downfall. Such habits tend to spread to other areas of your life as well. The seeds of success or failure in the later stages of life are often planted during your college days.

Many students are unhappy with their chosen degree program or the institute they are studying in. When negativity clouds your thinking, you're more likely to make misguided decisions that worsen the situation. Having confidence in your ability to improve your life at any point is crucial. Embrace what you currently have and systematically strive for improvement through small, positive daily choices. Take inspiration from the journey of Sundar Pichai, the CEO of Google. Although he initially wanted to pursue Electronics or Computers, he ended up in the Metallurgy branch. Despite this deviation, he gave his best and even received a silver medal upon graduation. He further pursued an MS in Material Science and an MBA from Wharton. Thereafter, his career skyrocketed at Google.

Satya Nadella, Microsoft CEO, graduated from a college that was not ranked very high in India. Similar stories abound, with individuals from diverse backgrounds making unexpected shifts to find success. For instance, I've seen graduates from Textile and Mechanical Engineering programs become faculty members in the Electrical Engineering Department by leveraging the flexibility of their coursework at the master's level. My spouse, too, started as a scientist but ended up teaching and conducting research in Mechanical Engineering. Moreover, I've seen a mining graduate who pursued a master's degree in computer science and subsequently joined Facebook (USA). These examples demonstrate that opportunities for growth and change exist beyond the constraints of your initial choices.

Importance of Good Company

You should actively seek out positive and happy friends. Studies have shown that our GPA tends to reflect the average of the group you associate with. By cultivating a strong desire for positive and happy companionship, you attract individuals who uplift your spirits, motivate you, and collectively enhance your academic pursuits.

Jim Rohn, the author and entrepreneur, said, *"You are the average of the five people with whom you spend the most time."* John Assaraf, a lecturer, entrepreneur, and behavior expert, wisely advises, *"I just do not hang around anybody that I don't want to be with. Period. For me, that's been a blessing, and I can stay positive. I hang around people who are happy, who are growing, who want to learn, who don't mind saying sorry or thank you... and [are] having a fun time."*

Shawn Achor, the famous author, said, *"Having great people around you can make you great and is even a better predictor of success than qualities like grit and resilience."* He also said, *"You actually achieve and perform better when you help others operate at their best. The majority of our potential, happiness, and everything was actually interconnected with the people surrounding us. We are more likely to excel and reach the heights of success by accepting the uplifting help from others and, in turn, reciprocating the assistance."*

Sports Advantage

Studies have consistently demonstrated that individuals who excel in sports and actively participate in them, even at the college level, are more successful [23]. This correlation can be attributed to the balanced perspective instilled by both victories and defeats in sports, which proves valuable in real-life situations. As mentioned earlier, sports also act as stress busters due to the physical activities involved. Moreover, participating in it for joy rather than competition creates bonhomie among the participants.

Shortcuts Can Be Harmful

As Gary Busey wisely stated, *"If you take shortcuts, you get cut short."* Small shortcuts are like free drugs offered by dealers to make you addicted and dependent on them. You may think copying assignments, lab reports, or even cheating during exams is an intelligent approach to student life. It often starts innocently but quickly spirals into a habit you grow to love. However, there is always a fear of getting caught and facing severe consequences. Even if no one else knows, you know you're taking shortcuts, creating internal disharmony, anxiety, worry, fear, and unhappiness.

Moreover, your self-esteem inevitably suffers because you recognize that you are engaging in improper actions and accepting incompetence. Additionally, whenever you encounter courses or teachers where such practices are impossible, you experience further disharmony. The result is lower grades, increased stress, and unhappiness.

If you habitually rely on shortcuts, you won't perform at the level your academic record suggests when you enter the job market or start a business. Driven by your obsession with achieving higher performance, you may feel compelled to seek shortcuts or cheat to demonstrate results despite lacking the necessary aptitude or capability. This dependence on shortcuts becomes a lifelong struggle. Even if you manage to deceive others and deliver results, you cannot find true happiness. Businesses cannot sustain themselves through continuous cheating. The resulting stress and worries will affect your professional life and seep into your personal life, straining relationships with family and friends. Ultimately, both your professional and personal lives will suffer.

A similar phenomenon occurs when you choose easy but not very useful courses. This choice leads to an addictive pattern, even though you may not consciously realize it. Even if you achieve good grades with such choices, your analytical, intellectual, and physical capacities diminish. You know you are taking an escapist route, but temptation overpowers you. This compromise leads to lower self-esteem and future worries. Job interviewers possess astute discernment in assessing your academic choices, which inevitably influences the selection process.

On the contrary, choosing to exert substantial effort in everything you do enables your mind and body to confront any challenge that comes your way. You can fulfill your duties with confidence, free from stress and worries. As a result, you achieve success in both your professional and personal lives. The best performers typically belong to this category.

You may believe that you know the type of job you will pursue in the future and select courses accordingly. However, this narrow approach is fraught with danger. Your perceptions of your desired job may change, and you may regret your course choices. Additionally, market conditions can shift, affecting the job landscape.Therefore, choosing broad-based courses is always safer.

In the next chapter, you will learn about time management skills.

• • •

CHAPTER XII

The Essence of Time Management

"Give me six hours to chop down a tree and I will spend the first four sharpening the axe." Abraham Lincoln

In time management, it is crucial to acknowledge that we cannot directly control time. We cannot hoard it for future use, exchange it, or regain it once it slips away. Each of us is allotted the same amount of time every day. However, what we can do is make the most effective use of the time we have. This necessitates setting goals, breaking them into actionable steps, and executing them efficiently.

"Time is really the only capital that any human being has, and the only thing he can't afford to lose." Thomas Edison

To elevate our overall well-being, we must prioritize our time and learn to say "no" more often, both to people and to tempting distractions. This means focusing on the activities that truly matter to us while letting go of those that do not align with our goals.

It is essential to simplify our lives and slow down. The encouraging news is that accomplishing less, rather than constantly striving for more, does not have to come at the expense of success. J. P. Morgan, a highly successful and innovative entrepreneur, once remarked, *"I can do a year's work in nine months, but not in twelve."*

Since time is a precious resource, we need to be like a businessman in using it in terms of prudent allocation, efficient utilization, and regular auditing.

Before delving into goal setting, planning, and time management techniques, it is imperative to cultivate a joyful and positive attitude. Such an attitude is the wellspring of willpower, motivation, and discipline.

Understanding Goals and Their Significance

Goals are the manifestation of our desires and dreams. They provide us with targets to focus on, infuse our lives with meaning and purpose, and empower us to control our destinies. Setting goals not only motivates us but also enhances our self-confidence. After all, hitting a target we cannot see is impossible. Therefore, goals are vital for personal growth and achievement. Remarkable individuals throughout history have been outstanding dreamers.

The purpose of having goals is to enhance our present experience. Goals serve as means, not just ends. They enable us to find fulfillment and satisfaction in the journey to our goals. It is important to recognize that as we mature and gain experience, modifying or changing our goals is perfectly normal. There is no need to become emotionally attached to specific goals.

A wise Japanese proverb asserts, *"Vision without action is a daydream and action without vision is a nightmare."*

Before embarking on setting professional and other types of goals, it is crucial to understand our Life Goals.

Life Goals

The ultimate aspiration is to sustain continuous joy in everything we do in every moment of our lives. The key to achieving this is wholeheartedly giving our best effort and approaching every task joyfully.

Personal Goals

As discussed in previous chapters, it is essential to prioritize activities that maintain the optimal state of our bodies and minds. Allocating time properly for these endeavors is of utmost importance. Developing healthy sleeping habits is critical for efficiently recharging our bodies and minds. Rising early gives us a sense of power and discipline throughout the day. Beginning the day, relaxed set the stage for a significant victory.

Other personal goals encompass personality development, hobbies, and relationships:

Certain qualities are universally valuable in personality development, whether in professional contexts or relationships. These qualities often outweigh talent and skills, providing a reliable and stable foundation for happiness and success. Such characteristics include integrity, honesty, loyalty, respect, trust, responsibility, humility, compassion, fairness, forgiveness, authenticity, courage, generosity, perseverance, kindness, lovingness, optimism, reliability, conscientiousness, and self-discipline.

You can prioritize the qualities you wish to cultivate. With regular and deliberate practice, you can improve in any area you choose.

Professional Goals

Self-awareness is crucial for attaining professional goals. Understanding our strengths, weaknesses, passions, aspirations, fears, and frustrations is essential. Regularly asking reflective questions and patiently recording our thoughts are integral to this process.

The next step involves developing an integrated view of our personal and professional goals, encompassing long-term, medium-term, and short-term aspirations. These goals must align with one another to avoid stress and inefficiency. Medium and short-term goals are sub-goals and milestones on the road to long-term goals.

Long-Term Goals

Long-term goals span a period of 5 to 15 years. These goals can be further broken down into 1 to 5-year goals, representing our ideal aspirations within a given timeframe. It is important to note that at this stage, the focus should not be on the specific path to achieving these goals. Instead, explore various possibilities and aspirations for all areas of life, including professional, health and fitness, family, social relationships, hobbies, personal qualities, and spiritual growth. Long-term goals evolve, and it is crucial to approach them with patience and persistence. It is perfectly normal for these goals to change as we gain more information, wisdom, and maturity. Therefore, having broad-based goals is essential, and the process of goal setting should be enjoyed in its entirety.

Since long-term goals require time to unfold, it is vital not to delay setting medium and short-term goals. The latter is relatively easier to define. For example, a semester study goal could involve achieving a certain SGPA or earning a specific grade in a particular course while gaining in-depth knowledge of essential subjects.

Academic Goals

Academic goals revolve around learning how to learn effectively, developing analytical and problem-solving skills, acquiring sound theoretical knowledge, and gaining practical experience. It is crucial to understand that while a CGPA may open a few doors, the above factors continuously open many more.

It is important to understand that you are a unique individual with unique aspirations. Hence, you need not copy the goals of even successful people. However, there is no harm in understanding the process from others.

The Process of Goal Setting

It is advisable to follow the following goal-setting strategy to ensure effective goal setting. This strategy advocates setting Specific, Measurable, Actionable, Realistic, and Time-bound goals. It is important to consider the motivation behind each goal, why it is important, and how it will impact your life. As the time frame for goal achievement increases, uncertainty in available data also grows. Accepting this reality is key. Imperfect plans are better than having no plans at all. Plans tend to improve with experience and wisdom. Maintaining a separate diary or using electronic devices such as a PC, laptop, or smartphone to record goals and progress is essential for easy access and monitoring.

Allocate specific time slots each day for developing or reviewing short-term plans. Utilize weekends and holidays for medium-term plans and take advantage of vacations or semester breaks for developing long-term plans.

Approach goals in each area one at a time. Explore multiple options for each goal. This process may be daunting for beginners due to a lack of experience, but do not worry if answers do not come immediately. Persevere and seek guidance from happy and successful seniors. Clarity will gradually emerge, and you will begin to enjoy the process.

Vague goals, such as desiring a great job, acquiring wealth, academic success, or physical fitness, should be made more specific. Define the type of job, salary package, position, and desired time frame. Decide on the desired CGPA, SGPA, and grades in specific courses. Furthermore, determine the level of knowledge you wish to attain in each course, whether it involves design, problem-solving, or simply exposure. In terms of health, set fitness and weight goals within a given period.

Throughout this goal setting exercise, it is important to be realistic, considering your current circumstances, capabilities, and constraints like health. Strive for continuous and incremental improvements rather than aiming for sudden leaps, as the latter often leads to pain.

Long-term goals can be ambitious if the short-term plans are incremental. This approach reduces resistance in the brain and fosters confidence.

Remove Distractions

Warren Buffet's advice on goal prioritizing [23]: *"First, you write down a list of 25 career goals. Second, you do some soul-searching and circle the five highest priority goals. Third, you take a good hard look at the twenty goals you didn't circle. These you avoid at all costs. They are what distract you; they eat away time and energy, taking your eye off the goals that matter more."*

Warren Buffet said: *"The difference between successful people and really successful people is that the really successful people say 'no' to almost everything."* These are the things on low priority.

Steve Jobs also said: *"I am actually as proud of the things I haven't done as the things I have done. Innovation is saying 'no' to a thousand things."*

Fascinating research on goal setting and achievement for four groups indicates that different strategies yield varying results [19]. The first group merely thought about their goals, while the second group wrote them down. The third group wrote down their goals and shared them with positive friends and relatives. The fourth group employed all these techniques and monitored their goal-setting and progress during execution. Unsurprisingly, the fourth group achieved the best outcomes.

Medium and Short-Term Goals

Creating a roadmap of shorter, more attainable milestones is crucial to breaking down long-term goals into manageable steps. These milestones provide clarity regarding the process, required resources, and efforts. Moreover, achieving these smaller sub-goals instils confidence and progress, building momentum for the overall journey. Integrating long-term goals into medium and short-term ones allows for checking the alignment and harmony among all three levels. This process creates monthly, weekly, daily, and hourly to-do lists. Completing these smaller goals provides a sense of accomplishment, boosts confidence, and improves momentum.

Timeline

Strict deadlines play a vital role in implementing goals effectively. They provide a framework for strict monitoring and feedback, ensuring progress and accountability.

Focus on Effort, Not Outcome

Making the goal-setting process centered around effort rather than the outcome is essential. Our effort is within our control, while the outcome depends on various complex factors. Outcome goals indicate where we want to reach, but the focus should primarily be on our effort. It is crucial to avoid vague goals and make them specific to facilitate clear action.

Avoid Action Paralysis

Striking a balance between goal setting, planning, and action is vital. Overemphasis on planning without action can lead to inaction and stagnation. It is essential to start with an imperfect plan, take small steps, overcome inertia, learn from experience, and refine the plan.

Keep Going

Challenges and obstacles are inevitable throughout the goal-setting process. It is crucial to persevere, seek help when needed, take breaks and rest when tired, and be open to trying different strategies if previous ones are not yielding results.

Celebrate

Developing a habit of celebrating milestones appropriately

after completing goals is important. Patting yourself on the back or marking completed tasks are simple acknowledgments that can be meaningful for smaller goals. Consider rewarding yourself with a treat, dinner, or a movie for more significant achievements. Find what works best for you, and incorporate the rewards into your plan, as they provide a psychological boost.

Review Performance versus Goals

Regularly reviewing and comparing your actual performance with the planned goals is crucial. This evaluation can be done daily, weekly, and monthly. Analyze and write down comments to understand any deviations from the planned outcomes and consider the reasons behind them. This analysis helps in course correction and guides future planning.

Major Review

After completing significant goals, it is important to conduct a thorough review of both the planning process and the execution. Evaluate whether the plans were too ambitious or lenient and learn from the experience. Sometimes, revising or discarding goals partially or entirely may be necessary.

Starting with simpler goals you believe you can achieve is advisable in goal setting. This minimizes resistance and fosters better progress. As you gain confidence and momentum, gradually take on more challenging goals.

Go with the Flow

Maintaining a balance between enjoying the process and keeping the end goal in mind is crucial. Be open to modifying goals if necessary and remain flexible. Avoid becoming overly attached to achieving a goal, as excessive emotion can lead to fear and stress.

Keep Decision-Making Process Simple

Every day, we have to process thousands of decisions. Too many choices not only spoil you but also leave us exhausted. Hence, it is good to decide an evening before about many things like 'what to wear, what to eat.' Our brain finds it difficult to decide what to do right now, rather than what to do later.

Steve Jobs learned the power of simplicity from Zen Buddhism, and wore a black T-shirt daily to avoid choice.

Semester Planning

Integrating semester planning allows for connecting semester, monthly, weekly, and daily study plans. This ensures optimal planning and creates a cushion to accommodate any slippages by incrementally redistributing lost hours over a longer duration. It helps prevent the need for panic and excessive workload accumulation towards the end of the semester.

The first step in semester planning is estimating the required study effort. This estimation improves with experience but should be initially based on a rough estimate. List all academic workload for the semester, including the number of theory courses, labs, assignments, projects, etc. Break down the study hours required for each topic in theory courses, taking into consideration reading, note preparation, and comprehensive understanding. Seek guidance from teachers, teaching assistants, and seniors if needed.

Similarly, determine the number of problems to be solved for each chapter in problem-solving courses, as well as the time required. Identify the workload and time frame for lab reports, quizzes, and tests. If there are assignments or group projects, allocate time accordingly.

After obtaining the total semester effort, divide it into

blocks leading up to each exam. Be mindful that the workload tends to increase towards the end of the semester due to numerous completion activities. It is a common mistake for students to wake up late and procrastinate. By working in a planned manner, you can distribute the workload evenly and avoid unnecessary stress.

Next, divide the monthly workload into weekly study requirements and break it into daily tasks, considering weekdays, weekends, and holidays.

In addition to academic commitments, make sure to allocate time for other activities such as relationships, meditation, exercise, sports and games, hobbies, clubs, competitions, recreation, social media, phone calls/chats, and personal or spiritual activities. Consider the minimum and maximum time required for each activity daily or weekly.

Perform an availability analysis by listing your daily occupied hours, including sleep, morning routines, meals, classes (lectures, labs, tutorials), and transit time. These are generally non-negotiable. Reserve additional cushion time of one hour per day on weekdays and three hours on weekends or holidays for contingencies. Subtracting these occupied hours from the total available hours provides the time you can dedicate to planned activities.

Record your utilization of free time daily for a week to gain insight into your habits and adjust as necessary.

Final Planning

Now, add the minimum number of hours for planned activities other than studying. You can also list desirable hours for some of these activities if desired. Subtracting these hours from the available hours will give you the total hours available for studying each day.

You may notice that the required planned study and

available hours do not match. Start adjusting the study hours per day based on the available time. If you feel comfortable with the time availability, you can allocate more hours to activities you are passionate about. However, remember this is a conscious tradeoff between activities based on your priorities.

Exercise caution when allocating time for clubs, positions of responsibility, special relationships, competitions, and events. Maintaining balance is crucial, and prioritizing based on values should be the foundation of your planning and time management. Be mindful not to fall into the trap of CV enrichment by simply adding numerous activities without excelling in them. It is better to focus on a few areas and showcase expertise.

In general, the number of available study hours is often less than what was initially contemplated. This requires a tradeoff between different study components and among various courses based on individual comfort levels. Not all courses and topics are equally difficult; the same applies to other components such as problem-solving, assignments, and projects.

Multiple iterations are necessary to arrive at a satisfactory plan for execution. However, it's important to understand that this plan can change with experience and unforeseen circumstances. Never compromise on the minimum number of hours allocated to each component, not just academics, and strive to reach the desirable hours whenever possible.

This exercise may initially seem daunting for those accustomed to a more carefree approach. However, as you begin implementing it, you will see its significant benefits. It's important to recognize that you don't have to become an expert in planning overnight. Every small step in this planning and time management process contributes to your experience and growth.

Detailed Daily Planning

Finally, allocate the available time for each day into different components, whether academic or otherwise. For academic activities, it is crucial to break them down into 15-minute blocks and list specific tasks for each block. Ensure that the necessary resources, such as books and notes, are available before the designated time slot.

Execution

As the day progresses, you may encounter slippages in different components. Depending on urgency and importance, you can decide which tasks to include in the cushion hours. As the week unfolds, you might notice accumulated slippages. Check if you can accommodate them during the weekend cushion hours. If not, you may need to adapt by re-planning the remaining days of the week.

When you realize that time is insufficient for a planned activity, it is important not to infringe upon other time blocks. Otherwise, the entire planning may become chaotic. It may mean allocating less time for theory study or reducing the number of problems to solve.

Handling Contingencies

Unforeseen events, such as illnesses or unplanned home visits, are sometimes inevitable. Accommodating them within cushion hours may not always be feasible. In such cases, it may be necessary to redistribute the slippages over a longer time frame by re-planning the remaining days, weeks, or even months. This ability to adjust and redistribute without panic allows minimum disruption to daily plans, providing a sense of control and improving confidence and efficiency.

Plans and Execution Are Not Perfect

It is important to acknowledge that planning and execution are not always perfect, and there are factors beyond our control. However, it is crucial not to give up. Following the approaches outlined in this book, you will remain on track and gain valuable feedback. Remember, chaos ensues when nothing is planned, but you can navigate challenges effectively with a structured approach.

Overcoming Procrastination

Procrastination, the act of delaying tasks, is a common struggle among college students that can harm their well-being. It increases stress levels, compromises the immune system, disrupts sleep patterns, and decreases happiness. The underlying cause of this issue lies in having a weak and untrained mind. However, implementing the practical strategies outlined in this book will enable you to tackle procrastination head-on and significantly improve your productivity.

Studies have consistently shown that prioritizing tasks in the present moment is synonymous with success, whereas procrastinating by saying "later" or "tomorrow" is synonymous with failure.

Next, the upcoming chapter focuses on getting the most out of the lectures you attend.

• • •

CHAPTER XIII

The Power of Class Attendance

"80% of success is showing up." - Anonymous
Research and experience have shown that students who consistently outperform their perceived capabilities across all academic disciplines possess a unique ability to attend every class sincerely. They attend classes regardless of their perceived relevance to their future aspirations or the quality of the teacher. These individuals often go on to achieve greater success in life. In light of this, you need to affirm the following every day:

"I love attending all my classes with joy because this habit is crucial for enhancing my capabilities. The ability to attend classes joyfully, even when others find them boring, is a strength that brings me immense satisfaction. Every class offers something valuable to learn, which greatly aids my studies. Even if a teacher lacks effective teaching skills, I focus on the content and strive to understand it to the best of my ability. This approach helps me become self-reliant, a highly beneficial quality for future employment and life."

Accept that there may be teachers, subjects, or topics you don't particularly like, and acknowledge any areas where you feel you are not proficient. Be at peace with your feelings. Then, ask yourself, "While all this may be true, what do I choose? Do I want to take small steps towards improvement and move closer to my goals, or do I allow things to deteriorate and distance myself from my objectives?"

When you lack the motivation to attend a class, ask yourself, "Will bunking this class help me move closer to my goals or take me further away from them?" Then, coax your mind into attending the class just for that day. The idea is to take up an incremental challenge, overcome inertia, and halt negative momentum. Even a single missed class can make it more difficult to grasp the next one.

Even when feeling slightly unwell, such as experiencing a mild headache, a cold, or a bad mood, try to attend classes as much as possible. If you're still unwell after a while, you can leave the class after explaining the situation to the teacher. This practice instills discipline and builds resilience by overcoming minor adversities. It doesn't matter if you don't fully understand the lecture; it is important to focus on taking notes. Continuity of good habits is the key. When you miss a class, it can trigger a negative chain reaction. Missing a single class may not seem like a significant issue, but it can lead to difficulties in comprehending subsequent lectures. This, in turn, may tempt you to skip future classes. Each instance of missing a class can negatively impact your mood, as guilt and negative thoughts can spread to other aspects of your life.

If you find it challenging to concentrate during a class, coax your mind into focusing for just ten minutes. If you feel comfortable, extend that time by another ten minutes, and so on. You may encounter resistance by asking your mind to focus for the entire class. However, concentrating for shorter periods is more agreeable to your mind

Maintain a Positive and Joyful Attitude

Our objective is to seek harmony in all aspects of life. Therefore, even if you dislike a particular course, affirm to yourself, "I love this course," before going to sleep, waking up, and just before the class begins. Similarly, even if you dislike a teacher, affirm, "I love [teacher's name]." Express gratitude for the teacher's efforts. It is important to note that these affirmations are about the desired states, not necessarily the present ones. You are visualizing yourself already in that desired state. This practice is part of the happiness approach applied to the task.

Visualize yourself attending classes with happiness and a smile on your face. You can even imagine yourself asking questions during the class, boosting your confidence.

Plan for Class Attendance

Often, students don't pay much attention to their appearance. However, looking presentable makes you feel good and attracts positive attention from others. Wear clean, smart clothes and shoes to lift your spirits and boost your confidence. Looking sharp helps you think sharp.

Prepare for the next day's classes by organizing the respective notebooks, pens, and any other materials required, such as a water bottle, in your bag. Decide in advance which clothes and shoes you will wear and have them ready. These small measures save precious time before the first lecture and mentally prepare you for attending classes.

Joining a group of like-minded students who prioritize attending all classes is an excellent habit. The positive energy within such a group is contagious.

Although many students may be present in the classroom, teaching and learning is ultimately an individual exchange of energy and knowledge between the teacher and each student. Therefore, even with the same teacher, every student benefits differently. This discrepancy has nothing to do with intelligence but rather with everyone's attitude. Consequently, some students find a particular teacher and subject interesting while others do not.

Each row in the classroom possesses its energy. You can experiment with observing the difference in the front and last rows. Concentration is significantly better in the front row. Many students are apprehensive about sitting in the front rows due to the fear of being singled out for questions. However, it is advantageous to overcome this fear, as the benefits outweigh the perceived disadvantages. Whenever a question is posed, attempt to answer it, even if only partially. Alternatively, if you genuinely cannot answer, honestly inform the teacher. In my observations, students who sit in the front row strive to give their best, regardless of their academic ranking. Conversely, backbenchers often lack sincerity in focusing on the subject being taught and typically attend class solely to meet attendance requirements. They fail to realize that they are wasting precious time and cultivating a habit of indiscipline that may harm their professional careers.

Before a class begins, remind yourself to be curious and mindful. This mindset greatly enhances concentration and understanding. If you demand immediate understanding during the class, you may feel stressed. However, if you maintain a curious and mindful attitude throughout the lecture, understanding comes more naturally. It is a good habit to take 3-5 deep breaths to calm down the mind and improve concentration. Take a quick glance at the one-page lecture abstract you prepared during your home-studies for the previous lecture. Read a brief outline of the upcoming lecture (refer to the "Studies" chapter for guidance). This preparation boosts your confidence, as you will feel one step ahead of others.

While attending a class, adopt the mentality of a frontbencher who pays full attention to the lecture, regardless of where you are seated. Keep a warm smile on your face throughout the lecture. This approach is the most effective way of learning and enjoying the class. Make it a point to ask questions when appropriate. If not possible during the class, ask the teacher or teaching assistants at the earliest mutually convenient opportunity. This engagement with the subject and instructor enhances your learning experience and builds your confidence. Asking questions is a vital life skill that improves with practice. Don't feel foolish or ignorant when asking questions; don't worry about others' reactions. The quality of your questions will also improve over time. Developing this skill during your student life will pay enormous dividends in your professional career.

Responding to Questions

In our course, a highly experienced professor frequently posed questions to students, often proving their responses incorrect. This created a sense of fear among most students, causing them to avoid eye contact and keep their heads down. I consciously changed my approach after witnessing this distress for a few weeks. I began smiling and eagerly raising my hand whenever a question was posed. I did not know then that professors prefer to ask questions to those who are hesitant rather than those who are eager to answer. This strategy provided me with additional time to contemplate my response and allowed me to identify the flaws in other students' answers. As a result, often, I was able to approach the correct answers through logical reasoning. Even when I was wrong, I found solace in maintaining a positive and confident mindset rather than succumbing to fear like the other students. This experience taught me a valuable lesson about the immense power of a positive attitude. Additionally, I noticed teachers' respect for students who regularly contribute answers. The confidence I gained from this practice naturally led me to ask questions and engage in meaningful discussions with all my teachers.

Develop Effective Note-Taking Strategies

Many students struggle with prioritizing understanding the material taught and taking detailed notes. It's rare to find individuals who excel in both aspects. Forming a small team with complementary qualities can be highly beneficial in such cases. Each member can focus on either understanding or note-taking and share their insights with the group. Use a dedicated notebook for each course and ensure proper spacing between your notes when note-taking. Even if teachers provide PowerPoint presentations for later reference, it is crucial to take brief notes in the form of bullet points. Most teachers prefer to elaborate on the bullet points during the lecture; you may miss valuable information if you don't note them. Be creative and enjoy the process of taking notes. Learn from students who are proficient in this art. Writing on paper not only aids memory recall but also helps minimize distractions in a noisy environment. While it may be tempting to record lectures using available technology, doing so often becomes a means to avoid concentrating on the lecture itself. Considering the limited time available for lectures daily, relying solely on recorded lectures puts you at a significant disadvantage. Concentrating and understanding the material later requires additional time and sincere effort. Merely attending classes to fulfill attendance requirements is a counterproductive mindset. Always strive to get the most out of each lecture and minimize the need for extensive catch-up efforts.

Eliminate Distractions

It is crucial to create an environment free from distractions during class. Your smartphone is often the biggest hurdle, so switch it off to avoid temptation. Additionally, kindly request your friends not to disturb you during class, and if necessary, distance yourself from them temporarily. Prepare If-Then rules in advance to handle any form of distraction. Research has shown that minor distractions like phone notifications or vibrations can significantly hamper concentration. Continually refocusing after distractions consumes valuable energy and negatively impacts the quality of your learning experience.

Find an Accountability Partner

Having someone trustworthy, such as a parent, elder sibling, or positive friend, to monitor your class attendance habits and hold you accountable can be immensely beneficial. This simple trick helps keep you on track and motivated to attend classes consistently.

Form a Supportive Group

Creating a group of like-minded and dedicated classmates who prioritize attending classes can greatly enhance your student experience. Consider traveling together for classes and supporting each other's attendance. The group can encourage them even when someone is not in the mood. Remember the saying, "A lone wolf dies, a pack survives."

Maintain Energy Levels

A balanced diet is vital in maintaining high efficiency throughout the day, especially in attending classes with focus and concentration. Start your day with a healthy breakfast and ensure a nutritious lunch. Minimize fast food consumption, as it is unsuitable for your body and mind. Stay hydrated throughout the day to maintain optimal energy levels.

On days when you have a series of classes and feel tired at the beginning of a new class, try to take 3-5 deep breaths. An affirmation like "I am peaceful and energetic" can also help. You may change it to suit your requirements at that moment. Additionally, consider keeping high-energy biscuits and a water or lemonade bottle in your bag for quick energy boosts.

Afternoon lectures following a meal can be particularly challenging in terms of concentration. Use your lunch break wisely by taking a short 5-10-minute nap if possible. These power naps can be highly refreshing. However, be cautious not to exceed 15 minutes, as you may feel groggy afterward.

Attending Tutorial Classes

These are primarily problem-solving classes based on the theory taught in lecture classes. Since this is a direct application of theory, the real understanding of the subject happens here. Hence, you must strive to attend all such classes and try to get the best out of them. This can be done by being aware of the relevant theory. Going through the tutorial sheet to be discussed in the next class in advance is good. If possible, try to solve as many problems as you can at least a day before so that you know where you need help. The tutorial class is best used to solve personal doubts or difficulties. It is necessary to check the correctness of your answers to the problems with the ones given by the teachers. If you still have difficulties after the class, seek answers from the teacher or TAs using any platform that is convenient to them. For more practice, ambitious students may ask for more challenging problems from the teacher.

Attending Practical Classes

These are laboratory classes where you are required to do some experiments mostly related to what is taught in theory classes. Most of these are hardware-related, but some are software-related as well. In the former, the training is to become familiar with the functioning of equipment and processes. In the latter, you are required to understand the detailed functioning of packages, programs, and algorithms. These are designed to give you the confidence to do things with your hand and make things work as desired. These also enhance understanding of some theory concepts. It is important to take an active interest in doing the experiment and trying to understand the logic. It is best done by being highly curious about everything. The more you ask, the more you learn.

Clarity about report writing style and overall expectations from the teacher is important. If you must form a group for the experiments, choose your mates who will share the workload and make the entire experience enjoyable.

Daily Attendance Audit

Spend a few minutes reflecting on your attendance for the day. Take note of what went well and what didn't, as well as the reasons behind missed classes. Consider strategies to improve your attendance and seek guidance from mentors if needed. This daily audit helps you stay mindful of your commitment to attending classes regularly.

In the next chapter, we will see how to study efficiently.

• • •

CHAPTER XIV

Embracing the Joy of Studies

"The wonderful thing about learning is that nobody can take it away from us." - B. B. King.

My forty years of teaching experience have shown me that students who consistently excel beyond their initial capabilities do so because of their passion for studies, regardless of whether they believe a particular course aligns with their aspirations. While this passion may vary among students, it can always be cultivated and intensified thoughtfully. In the following sections, we will explore two major aspects to help you practice joyful studying:

(A) Building up an approach for joyful studies. (B) Study Planning and Execution

Building up an approach for joyful studies

1. Transforming negativism to positivism

Engage in a daily dialogue with yourself, especially when you lack motivation or joy in studying. Remind yourself that you chose to be in this institute, that your studies are an investment in your future, and that you are committed to giving your best and making the most of the resources available. Even if you encounter a less-than-ideal teacher, empower yourself to become more self-reliant and put in extra effort. Embrace the habit of joyful studying, recognizing its importance in improving your knowledge base, analytical skills, and concentration. This habit forms the foundation for personal growth, confidence, wisdom, and happiness. Continually remind yourself of your commitment to overcome any obstacles during your studies.

When you find yourself lacking motivation, take a moment to write down the exact reasons for your resistance. Then ask yourself, "Do I choose to find solutions and improve my circumstances, moving closer to my dreams, or do I let things worsen, taking me further away?" Visualize a bright future from dedicated studies and the bleak and discouraging scenarios that may arise from poor study habits. Consider the difficulties of finding suitable employment or struggling in relationships, and let these contrasting visions motivate you.

If you don't feel like studying, coax yourself into doing it for just today. If the study session seems daunting, convince yourself to start and dedicate just five minutes to it. This simple act helps overcome inertia and builds momentum. If you feel comfortable, challenge yourself to continue for another five minutes, and so on. Remember to acknowledge your progress with positive affirmations like, "Good job! Keep it up!" Sometimes, instead of committing to a minimum time, you may read just a few pages or solve one problem at a time. By Starting small and celebrating each accomplishment, you can overcome mental resistance and build positive momentum.

If your concentration is lacking and affecting your study efficiency, try coaxing yourself to be curious and mindful for just five minutes. Start with this small timeframe and extend it for another five minutes if you feel comfortable. Acknowledge and reward yourself for each period of concentrated study by saying, "Good job! Keep it up!"

These incremental challenges effectively break down a large task into easily achievable and manageable sub-tasks. By completing these short tasks, you create a sense of reward, and it naturally motivates you to tackle more. This approach helps overcome resistance in your brain and mind, building positive momentum as you progress through your studies.

Before commencing any study session, doing a few minutes of deep breathing with closed eyes is useful. As mentioned earlier, it calms the mind and improves concentration, motivation, willpower, and discipline. It also provides increased Oxygen, which improves brain functioning.

Many students dislike studying because they struggle to understand concepts on the first attempt. However, it is important to remember that this is a common experience. Instead of becoming discouraged, approach your studies with curiosity and a desire to explore what each topic offers. Maintaining a lovingly mindful and curious attitude can significantly enhance efficiency and understanding. Affirm your intention to engage in mindful studying before sleep, waking up, and each study session.

Even if you don't enjoy studying in general or find a specific subject challenging, affirmations can help reshape your mindset. Repeat statements such as, "I love studying [course and topic]," or "I am improving in [course] every day."

2. Overcoming Phobia of Some Courses

Many students believe they are inherently bad at certain subjects, such as Math, and anticipate poor grades. Take inspiration from Shinzen Young's experience, as he struggled with math and science during his school years [4]. However, as a meditation expert later in life, he realized that his mind training could help him learn anything. To prove this to himself, he embarked on a journey of relearning math and science, starting from the 5th-grade level and gradually advancing to the graduate level. Throughout this journey, he discovered several helpful strategies:

- Improved concentration through meditation practice.

- The ability to study the same material repeatedly with unwavering focus until an understanding is achieved.

- Replacing negative self-talk with positive affirmations.

- Breaking down work into small, manageable chunks, celebrating each accomplishment to build confidence.

- Learning from the mindset of successful individuals and incorporating those elements into his approach.

If you struggle with remembering what you've studied, it is often a matter of attention rather than memory retention. By cultivating a positive mindset and implementing the tips mentioned above, you can gain the confidence to learn anything you desire, enhancing your chances of success.

3. Remain Energetic

Incorporating deliberate short breaks to reduce stress when studying for long hours is crucial. After every half-hour of study, take a two-minute break. During this break, stand up, stretch your arms and legs, take deep breaths with a smile, and engage in prayers or affirmations related to love, peace, or harmony. However, refrain from using your phone or internet during this period. After two hours of study, take a ten-minute break, during which you can go to the washroom and engage in the previously mentioned activities for slightly longer durations. After four hours of study, take a thirty-minute break, step outside, and go for a short walk in a peaceful area. You can also listen to music or check your mobile during this break. These measures improve your energy levels and mood and enhance your study efficiency.

(B) Study Planning

General planning

Before delving into specific study tips, ensure that you have a well-structured study module within your timetable, as suggested in Chapter 12. Your timetable should include all necessary details, including breaks during long study hours. The following recommendations are general guidelines that have proven useful to many students, but feel free to modify them according to your personal needs.

Maintaining a fixed study place and time whenever possible is beneficial, as it helps establish a positive habit. Keep your study area clean and free from distractions, ensuring that only the materials required for the specific study module are within reach. Adding a fresh flower or lighting an incense stick can also help create a conducive environment. If it aids your concentration, consider using headphones for noise cancellation or listening to music or songs. Some students find the library to be the best place for studying due to the complete silence and the presence of other dedicated students. While studying, keep your phone and laptop turned off and keep them as far away as possible. Studying alone is generally more effective, but you can seek help from friends to understand concepts or solve problems.

Before beginning each study session, refer to your daily study plan and write down the specific goals you aim to achieve during that period. These may include reading lecture notes and books, preparing concise summaries, solving tutorial or book problems, writing lab reports, or working on assignments or projects. Breaking down the time into fifteen-minute modules provides clarity and helps maintain focused attention. Take note of the resource materials, such as books or lecture notes, that you will use. Having this level of clarity improves your mood and overall efficiency. According to your plan, allocate your most cheerful and energetic hours to the tasks that significantly impact your desired outcomes.

Another important aspect is to strictly adhere to the allocated time for each study module, even if you cannot complete it to your satisfaction. Initially, this may seem unreasonable, but soon, you will realize the importance of completing tasks within the designated time frame as a matter of discipline rather than exceeding it and disrupting the schedule for other activities. As mentioned in the chapter on Time Management, you can modify future time allocation for the study modules based on the experience gained.

Regardless of your plan, it is beneficial to challenge yourself to complete tasks in slightly less time than expected. Strangely, activities tend to expand to fill the allocated time, so by accumulating saved time blocks, you can reward yourself with activities you enjoy. While you may not always succeed in completing tasks faster, the challenge improves your concentration. Based on your experience, you can adjust the level of challenge accordingly. This capability is not new to you; you demonstrate it during exam periods, albeit driven by stress and fear. The key is to learn to approach it joyfully whenever you wish.

Set aside time slots for seeking help from friends instead of interrupting your planned study time. By doing so, you can maintain a sharp focus and avoid distractions. It is best to keep your phone and laptop turned off and away from your study area during this period to avoid temptations. Inform your relatives and friends about your study hours, requesting them not to disturb you unless necessary. Discover innovative ways to avoid distractions, as you know your weaknesses and can address them effectively.

It is good to reassure yourself that you aim to do your best under all circumstances; therefore, you need not worry excessively about exam results.

Employing "If-Then Rules" helps overcome bad habits and distractions. For example, if you have an urge to check your phone, browse the internet, or play games, tell yourself to study for ten more minutes before indulging in those activities. If a friend invites you for a chat, game, movie, or shopping during your designated study time, politely decline and suggest another day. By diverting the intensity of momentary urges, you gradually develop a new identity as a disciplined individual, giving you a sense of pride in your achievements.

Now, let's explore specific strategies for different study tasks:

1. Lecture Notes/Abstract Preparation

During the allocated time for this task, review your recent class notes or listen to recorded lectures to enhance your understanding before the next class. Create a concise abstract of the lecture, limiting it to one page. Read through this abstract before the commencement of the next class.

To make studying easier, refer to books or additional materials. While reading, use a pen or pencil to run along each sentence without marking. Highlight or underline important points to enhance concentration and facilitate speed reading. Prepare fair notes using the highlighted material. As far as possible, this should be done modularly and immediately after the reading session. A separate notebook for each course is essential. Share and exchange good points with close friends to enhance everyone's understanding.

Simultaneously, prepare brief notes for quick revision before the exam. When studying derivations, maintain curiosity and mindfulness regarding the logic behind each important step. If any step is unclear, refer to the theory in the respective chapter or seek clarification from others.

Write explanatory comments for each significant step in the book. Reviewing these comments before the exam eliminates the need for memorization, allowing you to derive them effortlessly. Understanding derivations and problem-solving clarifies theoretical concepts significantly.

2. Solving Numerical Problems

Solving numerical problems is a crucial aspect of most engineering courses. It may seem challenging to some students initially, but with a smart work plan, persistence, and determination, you can learn to enjoy it.

You limit your growth potential if you favor easy topics and problems. Embrace the challenge of studying difficult topics and solving complex problems to enhance your potential. You have already experienced this during your entrance tests to this college.

Once you have a solid grasp of the concepts within a particular subject module, study solved problems from good-quality textbooks or lecture notes. Both theory and numerical problems are vital for understanding the subject matter. Next, attempt unsolved problems from books or tutorial sheets, starting with simpler ones and gradually progressing to more challenging ones. Before starting your study session, note which specific problems you intend to solve and the resources you need. Break the tasks into fifteen-minute modules to maintain focus and efficiency.

Initially, you may attempt problems independently but never hesitate to seek help from friends, teaching assistants (TAs), or teachers when necessary. Form a group of like-minded friends who can support and assist each other in all study matters. Collaborate on solving problems by distributing the workload among group members, ensuring everyone understands the solutions. This approach saves time and energy. Additionally, review previous exam papers for the course. While these papers may vary slightly depending on the teacher and content covered, most of the material remains the same. After you are satisfied with your problem solutions, create a brief note (algorithm) summarizing the essential elements of the solution process. Maintain a separate notebook, as it becomes a valuable resource. This preparation eliminates the need to solve problems right before the exam.

Some students find reading theory alone to be boring, making it challenging to transition to solving numerical problems. For such students, it is advisable to start directly with solved problems. As you encounter unfamiliar theoretical concepts, refer to the relevant theory. Then, progress to unsolved problems from books or tutorial sheets, beginning with simpler ones and identifying the necessary theoretical concepts as you go along. Another effective strategy is to obtain previous years' course papers and attempt to write answers for each question. Unlike in an actual exam, you can use books and notes, and there is no time limit. This approach enhances focus, generates interest, and increases motivation. This strategy was successfully employed by my batch mate, Pratik Jain, who faced frequent illnesses and had low-class attendance. Despite these challenges, he achieved top ranks using this method. I also benefited from following his approach.

Answering Descriptive Questions

When faced with a descriptive question in an exam, refer to your notes for guidance. The allotted marks and time should determine the length of your answer. To avoid the stress of memorizing complete answers, write your answers in bullet points that can be elaborated upon during the exam, depending on the time remaining. Memorizing bullet points is much easier, and when you have a solid understanding of the concepts behind each bullet point, writing in your own words becomes simpler.

Mock Tests

As you have already experienced during the entrance exams, Mock Tests are critical in preparing you for the real ones. These provide you with critical feedback about your preparation and what you lack. These must simulate actual ones as much as possible. Choose a location where you are completely undisturbed during the test period. Procuring such test papers is the first crucial task. Previous years' test papers from your institute are the easiest resource. However, wherever feasible, you may also seek such papers from other Institutes. Although the exact course contents and practices may vary significantly between different Institutes, one can always pick up selected questions on similar topics and prepare your mock test paper. Rather than an individual effort, a group effort is always desirable. It is important to note that the extent of effort you put into this would depend on your own goal regarding this course. After every mock test, you should analyze your performance and where to improve. The next test should only be taken after you have taken some improvement countermeasures. During these tests, you should develop a habit of preparing the sequence in which you will attempt the questions. When you commence the exam, spend a few minutes reading all questions first to assess the ones that are in increasing order of difficulty. The likely time estimate of solving each one should also be noted. Keeping these in view, you can prepare the exact sequence in which you would like to answer the questions. The strategy for Multiple Choice Question Papers is different.

Daily/Weekly/Monthly Review

At the end of each day, take the time to review your

performance against your study plan. Assess what went well and what did not, identifying the reasons behind both. Identify major and minor areas of concern and consider how to improve in each area. If you find it difficult to determine the best course of action, don't hesitate to seek guidance from mentors who can provide valuable insights. Repeat this exercise weekly and monthly to gain a longer-term perspective. These reviews will help you understand how to address any slippages that may have occurred. If certain strategies are not working, be open to making changes and trying new approaches.

Avoid accumulating excessive work, even if you have experienced some setbacks. Take note of the lessons learned from any slippages, but avoid being too hard on yourself. Instead, focus on what you can do from that point onwards. This principle applies to slippages due to health issues or other reasons. The trajectory of your performance over time is what matters most. Even small gains or losses can accumulate over a period. To assess your progress, evaluate yourself on a scale of 10 each week, considering how well you are doing concerning your study plan. It is a positive sign if your scores are consistently improving, even if only incrementally. However, if your scores are declining, it serves as a wake-up call for introspection and remedial action.

Handling Sickness

When you are unwell, prioritize taking loving care of yourself. Follow medical advice, take necessary medications, and ensure you get adequate rest. Maintaining a positive mindset is crucial, as it can lead to faster recovery. If your illness is mild, there is no need to abandon your studies completely. Engage in light activities such as reviewing your friends' notes, catching up on missed lectures, or studying easier topics you enjoy. Take breaks and work for short durations. It can also be helpful to have audio chats with classmates to stay informed about what you missed in each class. They don't need to be physically present; a simple audio conversation will suffice. Being aware of the content covered in your absence will give you confidence when you resume attending classes. Work on report writing or simple assignments to prevent a complete breakdown in study momentum and avoid accumulating a heavy workload.

The next chapter focuses on exam-related strategies.

• • •

CHAPTER XV

Cultivating a Joyful Exam Mindset

"Exams and grades are temporary; education is permanent." - Anonymous

Exams are an essential part of academic life. They play a crucial role in assessing your strengths and weaknesses and providing feedback for improvement. It would help if you looked forward to the exam as a valuable experience and training opportunity. Believe in your potential for success and, more importantly, your capacity for improvement. Anticipating the positive aspects of the exam triggers the release of endorphins, chemicals that promote happiness. See the exam as a step towards personal growth.

Before Exams

In addition to your regular Shutdown Routine, spend a few minutes before sleeping and in the morning following your Start-Up Routine to perform the following activities:

Before sleep, you should repeatedly affirm, "I love exams and am committed to doing my best."

Visualize the happiest day of your life and recall your best exam performance. Spend a few minutes singing, playing music, or reading a comedy article. Keep a collection of jokes, videos, and articles that uplift your mood. These activities will put you in a positive state of mind, optimizing your brain's performance.

Instead of praying for an easy question paper, which reflects a negative mindset, pray for the ability to do your best regardless of the question paper's difficulty. Practice mindful, deep breathing whenever possible. Walking meditation, where you count your steps or express gratitude with each step, can also be beneficial. The key is maintaining a calm, peaceful, and happy mind.

The exam preparation time for each subject is limited. Develop a smart study plan that allocates time for each subject and topic, considering theory and problem-solving. Strive to adhere to this plan as closely as possible. Based on prior planning, you may decide to omit certain topics entirely. Some topics may appear challenging or not have been covered due to time constraints, and avoiding attempting them shortly before the exam is acceptable.

View the short study period before the exam not as a deadline but as an opportunity to learn how to study efficiently in a limited time frame. Consider it excellent training for life.

Stick to your planned reading material on the day of the exam. Avoid reading until the last minute, as it creates unnecessary stress. You may feel you're absorbing more information, but it hampers your performance.

"Do what you can, with what you have, where you are." - Theodore Roosevelt

Regardless of your level of preparation, focus on what you can do from that point onward. Regard the exam as a means for personal improvement rather than a competition with others. Embrace it as a chance to make significant progress. Depending on your temperament, preparation, and confidence, decide beforehand which strategy suits you best for answering questions during the exam. Most students like to gain confidence by tackling the easier ones first.

Prepare "If-Then Rules" to handle various situations that may arise during the exam. These plans should be based on your experiences during studying and previous exams, addressing real-time contingencies. Create these rules when your mind is calm to prevent panic and poor decision-making in stressful exam situations. Adhere to these rules as much as possible. Some examples of such rules are as follows.

"If I get stuck while solving a question, I will first take a few deep breaths, pray for wisdom, and then quickly assess whether I should spend more time on it or move on to the next question."

"If I am short of time for some descriptive questions, I will first write down the answer in bullet points, leave enough blank spaces, and then elaborate as much as possible depending on the available time. For the problem-solving questions, I will provide as many steps in the answer as possible."

Avoid missing any exams for minor reasons. Challenge yourself to see how well you can perform despite any challenges. This approach helps develop a strong character.

During the Exam

Keep Body and Brain Energetic

On a stressful day like the exam day, your diet tends to suffer. However, for your brain to stay alert and energetic, maintain a balanced, energy-rich diet, especially during breakfast. Stay hydrated and energized by having water and lemonade during the exam. For long-duration exams, keep high-energy biscuits on hand. Adequate glucose levels are crucial for efficient brain function and overall happiness.

Prayers and Affirmations

Throughout the period leading up to the exam, maintain a positive mindset through prayers, affirmations, gratitude, and other techniques described in this article. Offer prayers for strength and wisdom to remain calm and perform your best in the exam. Before entering the exam hall, exchange pleasantries with everyone and genuinely wish your friends well.

In the Exam Hall

When the exam begins, refrain from reading any further. Relax and put a smile on your face. Look at everyone in the room with love and silently wish them well. Close your eyes and take a minute to engage in deep, mindful breathing. If you believe in God or find it helpful, pray or chant mantras. Affirm your intention to remain peaceful throughout the exam.

After receiving the question paper, don't rush to answer immediately. Read each question carefully with love and a smile on your face. Depending on the assessment of the questions, decide the order in which you would like to attempt the questions.

Remember your plan, including any memory tips you may have prepared for descriptive questions. Time management is crucial. Prioritize the questions and allocate appropriate time to each one. The goal is to maximize your marks with the available preparation. Attempt to answer as many questions as possible, even if you don't know the complete answer. Write partial answers to those questions. Mark the answered questions, compliment and reassure yourself that you are giving your best effort. If you get stuck on a question, calmly acknowledge it, take a few deep breaths, and move on to the next one. Avoid becoming emotionally attached to any question, which can hinder your progress. Remind yourself that you are doing your best under the circumstances.

For numerical problems, carefully note the data and the specific output required. Use the algorithms you prepared during your studies to solve such questions. Even if some questions seem difficult, note them and move on to others peacefully.

After solving each question, take a short break of a few seconds. Close your eyes, pray for wisdom, maintain a peaceful state, and remind yourself to stay mindful throughout the rest of the exam.

After the Exam

After completing the exam, regardless of how you think you performed, you must express gratitude to God and your teachers for the opportunity to receive feedback. Avoid rushing to compare answers with others. When you are peaceful and relaxed, take time later to analyze your performance. If you feel you have not done well in an exam, surrender it to God and ask for strength and wisdom to remain calm, optimistic, and energetic for the next one. Take a short nap if required. Close this chapter of the previous exam and shift your focus towards preparing for the next one.

• • •

CHAPTER XVI

Introduction to Joyful Research

"No research is ever truly complete. The beauty of good research lies in its ability to pave the way for something even better, often resulting in its own overshadowing." - Anonymous.

In this chapter, we will explore the challenges faced by research scholars, delve into attitude aspects, examine the detailed research process, and finally explore the art of idea generation and management.

A common misconception about research programs is that they focus solely on gaining expertise in a narrow field. However, developing expertise is only a part of the broader objective of learning how to conduct research effectively, which is crucial for long-term success. Employers often value this capability more than specific expertise, as it demonstrates your training in conducting independent research. It is important to remember this and strive to acquire a broad knowledge base while pursuing your research. Developing this capability should not be left until the end when seeking job opportunities.

Challenges

Research scholars often face significant stress and unique challenges among various groups of students. Unlike B. Tech and M. Tech degrees, which follow a structured format with fixed timelines, research programs are largely unstructured and open-ended, except for the maximum time limit. This freedom can lead to difficulties for some individuals. Since there is no fixed template, research scholars must rely on guidance from their seniors and supervisors. Unfortunately, not everyone is fortunate enough to receive such guidance. Additionally, the relationship between a research scholar and their supervisor is crucial for success, and if multiple supervisors are involved, the situation can become even more complex. Therefore, developing good public relations skills becomes essential.

Another challenge research scholars encounter is the uniqueness of each research problem. Furthermore, the supervisor's research capabilities and reputation, both within and outside the institution, can significantly impact the research output. Students often compare these factors, and those at a disadvantage may feel demotivated, attributing their struggles to bad luck. It is important to recognize that inequalities exist from birth, such as the country we are born in, our parents, their financial status, and our physical attributes. We must embrace the Serenity prayer and accept these inequalities in life and our research pursuits while striving to do our best. Non-acceptance only leads to suffering.

Many students embark on a Ph.D. program for the wrong reasons, such as seeking the highest degree as an honor or improved job prospects, without truly understanding whether they have an aptitude for research. Most individuals have little to no knowledge about conducting research or the factors that can significantly impact their experience. This chapter aims to inform research scholars of every aspect of the research process and provide guidance on navigating these challenges effectively.

Preparing for Joyful Research

Creativity resides within each of us, even if we fail to recognize it due to negative conditioning and stress. It is challenging for good and creative ideas to emerge when fear, tension, and anxiety dominate our minds. Unlike other professions, creativity thrives in a peaceful and happy mind. To excel in research, bravery, courage, and training ourselves to be "creative" are essential skills that can be developed through practice.

Gratitude for the opportunity to engage in creative work is paramount. Remember, success or failure should not define your self-worth; your dedication to the work truly matters. Focus on cultivating a love for research, even if you may not feel it now, as this love can be nurtured through practice.

The foundation of creativity lies in having faith and belief in your creative abilities and continuously working on improving them. Creativity is not consistent in output, and extended periods of apparent fruitlessness can be disheartening if you fail to understand and accept the nature of the work. Surrounding yourself with happy friends who support and inspire one another is crucial. Take a genuine interest in their work, teach each other, and learn from their experiences. Recognize that not everyone excels in every aspect, emphasizing the importance of synergy and collaboration. This collaboration has a multiplier effect on the quality and quantity of your work.

Now, let's delve into the process of conducting research.

Selecting a Research Topic

Selecting a research topic can be one of the most daunting tasks, especially if your supervisor does not provide direct guidance or assistance. The vast areas and extensive literature can easily overwhelm you if you approach it without a systematic and enjoyable method. However, there is an advantage to not having your topic predetermined by a supervisor—it grants you the freedom to choose a topic that aligns with your interests and strengths. Embrace this opportunity as a boon. Some supervisors intentionally provide this freedom to encourage independent thinking. Here are the steps to guide you through this process:

1. Discuss possible research topics with your supervisor and seniors for a week or two. Additionally, glance through top journals to review paper titles and get an idea of the latest activity in various areas. You don't need to read the papers in detail at this stage. Based on this exploration, select a few topics for further investigation.

2. Focus on one topic at a time and create a list of around 20 related papers. Read the abstracts and introduction of these papers and take notes on important points, such as the problem addressed, significant contributions, and the overall achievement process. Depending on the area of research, include details about techniques, tools, mathematical models, and processing. After going through this process for each topic, write down your thoughts on how much you like each one and assess your confidence in the required background skills. Repeat this exercise for the other topics as well. This comprehensive process may take up to two weeks. Finally, take some time to decide on the final topic for your work, keeping your supervisor informed along the way. As supervisors are often busy, utilize email communication to share your progress. It is crucial to understand that there is no perfect answer to selecting the best research topic, and that's okay. The process is subjective, and you should be content with what resonates with your conscience. Surrender the final decision to a higher power and proceed.

3. After selecting a topic, embark on a rigorous literature review. However, it is important to approach this step systematically to avoid overwhelming yourself with information. Begin with the list of papers identified in Step

2. Read each paper with a focus on gaining awareness rather than complete understanding. Create one-page notes for each paper, summarizing the problem addressed, significant contributions, key concepts involved, and other relevant details related to the research area. Repeat this exercise for each paper on your list.

4. Review all the one-page summaries Once you have completed this exercise. With your supervisor's guidance, shortlist about six to eight papers most suitable for your work.

5. Conduct a more detailed reading for each paper shortlisted in Step 4 to understand the processes behind the contributions. However, even at this stage, the goal is not to gain a complete understanding. Create a 2-3-page abstract for each paper, including details about the techniques, tools, processes, mathematical models, and complexity based on their relevance to your research area. Share this review with your supervisor and shortlist 3-4 papers together for a final thorough review.

6. Read each paper listed in step 5 as if you were planning to implement the research yourself. Take your time to understand all the complexities involved. Consult additional background material to enhance your understanding of the research topic if necessary.

Background Preparation

Develop a strong background in the selected research problem. Now that you understand the requirements of this area, work with your supervisor and seniors to create a detailed plan for building the necessary expertise. Depending on your research area, this may involve learning to use specific instruments, familiarizing yourself with lab processes and reactions, programming, mathematical models, and analytical tools. If possible, attempt to replicate a small work previously conducted by other researchers or your senior colleagues to gain confidence and a deeper understanding of your chosen research topic.

The Process of Problem Selection

Problems exist everywhere, and recognizing them is the first step. Problems stimulate our thinking and inspire us to seek improvements, leading to the emergence of new ideas. Observe the difficulties you encounter in your daily work and consider possible solutions.

Review papers authored by experts in the chosen research topic offer crucial insights into the industry's challenges and the solutions it needs. Furthermore, the literature reviews found in reputable journals within the same field shed light on the areas where the research community places high value on contributions.

Begin by selecting a problem within your capabilities, focusing on where you can excel using your existing knowledge and skills. Gradually challenge yourself to tackle problems slightly beyond your comfort zone, having confidence in your ability to learn the necessary skills.

Incubating New Ideas and Their Management

Truly great ideas are not born out of sudden inspiration but through a process. Each day, an individual observes and works diligently to nurture hunches, which can eventually transform into full-fledged ideas.

We often hear about successful ideas but seldom witness the weeks, months, or even years of labor and early failures that preceded that success. The human mind seeks the path of least effort in everything we do. Instead of generating numerous ideas to explore, we often desire to identify just the "best" one, hoping to conserve energy. This approach is flawed. Even if we come up with an idea, we cannot determine its true potential without investing time and effort to understand how it will work. We can discern whether it is good only through dedicated work on an idea. The following example shows how quantity can lead to quality.

After a week, one group was asked to submit their best photograph in a photography-related study. The second group was tasked to take 100 photographs and submit the best one after a week. Surprisingly, the second group produced the best results because they kept on improving through the experience with the previous ones. They had ample opportunity to do the same. The first group, obsessed with the best quality, did not experiment enough. The lesson here is that the best should not be the enemy of the good.

Ideas come to us in random bursts. Some days, we may generate many ideas, while on other days, not a single idea may surface. Among these ideas, some may initially seem average or even poor, leading us to reject them instinctively. However, with further exploration, such ideas can develop into excellent ones. Ideas that are truly exceptional from the beginning are rare occurrences.

On any given day, we have an average of fifty thousand thoughts. It is normal for most of these thoughts to be forgotten, as our brains naturally filter out unnecessary information to maintain our sanity. The challenge is that we often forget many good ideas along the way unless we consciously try to record them.

Interestingly, good ideas emerge when our minds are relaxed, such as during a walk or showering. In this state, our brains establish connections between different neural pathways, facilitating the development of new ideas. However, due to the relaxed nature of our minds, we often neglect to jot down these ideas. Therefore, it is essential to keep recording tools within easy reach to capture these fleeting moments of inspiration.

Review Ideas from Time to Time

To further develop your ideas and transform them into something significant, it is important to review them regularly. Allocate time at least once a week to assess your ideas. During this review, you can filter out less promising ideas, organize others, and start developing potentially successful ones. It is also beneficial to look beyond your discipline for inspiration and discuss with friends from different fields. Their perspectives can offer valuable insights and help you find innovative solutions.

Production Phase

At any given time, it is advisable to have a mature, well-developed idea into which you are putting maximum effort, with the expectation of promising results. Simultaneously, it is essential to have a backup problem that you have contemplated and requires further work before actual implementation. Additionally, maintain a list of promising problems that need more in-depth thinking. When encountering severe bottlenecks in your primary problem, assess whether it is a short-term issue that can be resolved by re-planning your activities or a long-term challenge. For short-term snags, utilize free time for activities that couldn't be addressed due to work pressure, such as pending paper writing, literature review, or learning skills relevant to your work. If the difficulties are long-term, consider shifting your focus to the next promising problem. In short, keep a To-Do list that is long enough to ensure you are never short of engaging and fulfilling work.

Tips About Paper Writing

Learning the art of paper writing should start early during the initial literature survey phase. Keep a journal and take note of how well-known researchers write their papers. Observe the writing style of experienced seniors within your research group as well. Note how each section is written, from the Abstract to the Conclusion. Some editors and reviewers may have specific preferences for certain writing styles, which you can learn through experience.

Some renowned authors suggest reading the best papers and then attempting to rewrite them without referencing the original versions. This exercise helps in developing logical and artistic aspects of paper writing. Afterward, compare your rewritten version with the original paper to identify areas where the author excelled.

Avoid making exaggerated claims about your work. Instead, adopt a modest tone while highlighting the strengths of your research based on factual evidence.

Selecting the Journal for Submission

During the literature survey, you will gain insights into the types of work published in various journals. With guidance from your supervisor, create a ranking of journals in your research area. Collaborate with your supervisor to evaluate the suitability of your work for different journals. If you believe your work is of excellent quality, aim for top-tier journals, especially in the initial phases of your research. Even in the case of paper rejection, the feedback received can contribute to better-quality research. Select a journal based on its ranking and how your work aligns with its scope as much as possible. This approach helps avoid the time delays associated with multiple journal reviews before rejection. However, the final decision regarding the level of risk you are willing to take is entirely up to you.

Reviewers and Editors provide an immense service to researchers without monetary compensation. They also carry a substantial workload. Therefore, expressing gratitude towards them and praying for their welfare is important to foster a harmonious relationship instead of an adversarial one. Include this expression of gratitude in your daily schedule, particularly during the paper review phase. Any negativity towards reviewers and editors only increases the likelihood of paper rejection.

Understanding the Review Process

It is crucial to understand that the review process is imperfect, and you may not always receive fair treatment. Some reviews may seem misguided or overly critical, while others may offer valuable insights from knowledgeable reviewers. Overall, the feedback received can contribute to the improvement of your work. Regardless of the nature of the feedback, it is important not to become emotionally attached to your work.

Most journals require multiple rounds of review before accepting a paper. Therefore, patience is necessary. Different journals have varying time cycles for reviews, and seeking feedback from your research group can provide insights into these timeframes. Consider this information when selecting a journal for submission.

Responding to the Reviewer's Comments

Upon reading the reviewer's comments for the first time, it is natural to perceive them as biased or incorrect due to emotional involvement. Take a second look at the comments after a day or two when you are in a calmer state of mind. Write down each point and, giving the benefit of the doubt, try to understand the reviewer's perspective. Upon deeper reflection, you will realize that the reviewer often has genuine concerns. Avoid rushing to resubmit the paper. Instead, review your response multiple times, seeking ways to improve it further. The best strategy is to address the reviewer's suggestions as much as possible rather than aggressively justifying your initial approach unless you have significant and logical justifications to support it.

Facing Paper Rejection

Your paper may face rejection during the first review or after subsequent rounds of review. Regardless, your primary focus should always be engaging in joyful research, submitting your work for evaluation, and embracing the learning process. This mindset ensures that the reward lies in the pursuit of knowledge and growth rather than solely in acceptance or rejection.

Facing Uncertainty

Uncertainty is an inherent part of a research scholar's life. Embrace it as a friend that helps you evolve into a better and stronger individual. When you let go of resistance and remain relaxed, you can adapt to any situation and perform at your best. Train yourself to face uncertainty by regularly using mind-programming affirmations and prayers designed to instill confidence in your ability to handle uncertainty.

Psychological security is essential for fostering creativity. Keep your risk exposure within a comfortable range. Maintain optimism and ambition while having adequate safeguards against failures. Understand that not every idea will lead to significant breakthroughs. If your work is publishable in a decently ranked journal, do not discard it. However, always remain open to discovering better ideas and identifying reliable fallback options. Do not let the success of your Ph.D. or postdoc depend solely on a few ideas.

Facing Failure

Incremental research involves lower risks and rewards. However, if you aim for high-quality, impactful research, you must be prepared to face failure without being discouraged. Develop a habit of working modularly and maintaining detailed documentation, significantly aiding in managing failure. Regularly share these details with your supervisor and, if possible, with senior colleagues. This facilitates error detection and correction.

Knowing when to persevere after failures or let go of an idea you have invested significant time in is not easy, emotionally or intellectually. To make the best decisions in these situations, tap into your wisdom. Avoid questioning such decisions after encountering negative results because the larger life plan remains unknown. Remember, even great individuals have often experienced failure or lost battles.

When you have multiple ideas to work on, failure of some ideas does not hurt as much. Adaptability is a valuable trait for both successful businesspeople and research scholars.

Facing Imperfection

As mentioned earlier, imperfection exists to varying degrees in all aspects of life—administration, yourself, supervisors, colleagues, relatives, editors, reviewers, and Ph.D. thesis examiners. Accept this reality peacefully and strive to do your best in all circumstances. Non-acceptance only perpetuates the problem, creating a vicious cycle.

Managing Freedom

One unique aspect of a research scholar's life is the relatively higher freedom regarding time and activities. However, most of us lack the training to use this freedom best, which can lead to serious challenges. Recognize this fact early on to avoid future difficulties. The foundation for managing freedom lies in effective time management, which is discussed in detail in a separate chapter.

Preparing for Post-Ph.D. Job Opportunities
The long period of a Ph.D. offers valuable training beyond attaining the degree itself. This training is what ultimately secures a job, not just the degree. While specialization is important, learning how to learn is even more critical. The skills acquired during your Ph.D. are not limited to your specific research area but can be applied to various professional domains. To develop a broad knowledge base, go beyond the minimum course requirements and consider auditing additional courses. Even if the topics are not directly related to your research, familiarize yourself with mathematical models, computer packages, instruments, equipment, and processes relevant to other researchers in your field. Seek opportunities to teach small modules, as teaching is an excellent way to deepen your understanding. In addition to knowledge, excellent communication skills are vital for a successful career. Deliberately enhance your communication skills through lectures, report writing, and interpersonal interactions. Observe and learn from teachers and peers who excel in this area.

Developing a confident and pleasant personality should also be a goal. Cultivate good public relations skills, as they are crucial for professional growth. The internet and various books provide ample resources for achieving this objective.

Continuous improvement of your English language skills, which serves as the primary language of professional communication, is essential. People expect highly qualified individuals to have strong English proficiency, which is beneficial in various contexts.

Developing effective interview skills is crucial. Separate guidance on this topic is provided in the book since the job requirements in industry and academia differ significantly, along with the corresponding knowledge and skill sets. Stay in touch with your seniors in your field of interest and seek their advice and insights.

• • •

189

CHAPTER XVII

Turning Failures into Stepping Stones

"Success is not final; failure is not fatal: It is the courage to continue that counts." – Winston Churchill.

We all face failures in our professional work and personal relationships. Let's explore these separately.

"My past has not defined me, destroyed me, deterred me, or defeated me; it has only strengthened me." Dr. Steve Maraboli.

Failure in professional work

Sometimes, our performance in a project or task falls short of expectations. The degree of dissatisfaction may vary depending on various factors, such as the extent of underperformance and the stakes involved. Sometimes, we might even feel like failures. However, it's important to differentiate between failing to meet expectations and labeling ourselves as failures. There is room for improvement in the former, whereas we convince ourselves that we can't do any better in the latter.

If we observe the evolution of individuals or organizations, we realize that growth often occurs through failures. Everything requires trial and error before anything worthwhile is achieved, from learning to walk as toddlers to playing games, studying at various levels, or designing products.

Even highly successful individuals like Steve Jobs, Edison, and Jack Ma faced failures on their journey to the top, even after reaching the pinnacle of success. Their stories of how they dealt with failure can be a great inspiration. When we recognize that failure is a natural and inevitable part of life, we can embrace it as an opportunity to learn, grow, and become stronger and wiser.

In such situations, it's normal to experience initial feelings of pain, hurt, and anger because we haven't fully mastered the art of happiness. There's no need to be ashamed of these emotions, and we mustn't try to suppress them. Instead, we should accept what we feel without resistance or judgment. We can acknowledge the pain and allow it to pass away gradually. If the trauma is too intense, seeking professional help or considering medication to alleviate the distress is a valid option. The key in such situations is to avoid making any hasty decisions about our future course of action. It's best to make decisions with a calm and peaceful mind.

Regaining composure after a failure is crucial before deciding on the next steps. Engaging in meditation or mindfulness practices can help us find inner calm. Writing down our feelings about the situation can also help dilute the negativity we may harbor.

Once the initial pain subsides, it's time to analyze the situation. Although there may be a strong urge to blame others or circumstances for the failure, taking responsibility for our actions is important. However, even if we have made mistakes, we must not engage in self-bashing. Instead, we can apply the Serenity Principle and assess whether we did our best or could have done better in certain areas. Let's accept with serenity the things we cannot control.

There may be certain factors within our control that contributed to the underperformance. Was it due to insufficient preparation or excessive stress during the examination? Was the plan flawed, or did we struggle with time management? Did the study materials not suit our learning style, or did we lack practice in problem-solving?

If we don't feel a sense of competition with others, there's no reason to be ashamed. We can start by mentally complimenting those who performed better than us and then express our admiration personally. Let's observe how they prepare and answer questions, as building rapport with high achievers can be beneficial. We can also review answer books of students who performed well and compare our answers with model answers provided by teachers. Showing appreciation to teachers and teaching assistants for their efforts and wishing them happiness can foster positive relationships. It's important to be proactive in seeking help from all available resources, such as teachers and T.A.s. Patience and persistence in seeking guidance will pay off.

When you keep searching for ways to improve your situation, you stand a chance of finding them. When you stop searching, assuming they can't be found, you guarantee they won't.

Remember, we always have the power to make things worse or better. The choice is ours. Courage doesn't always roar; it can be a small voice that says, "Let's try again." Attitude is far more important than talent. Some armed forces and space agencies even refuse to recruit individuals who haven't experienced failure because the ability to bounce back after failure is crucial. In job interviews for higher management positions, it's common to be asked about a significant failure and how one bounced back to achieve an even better position.

The Significance of Mentors and Positive Relationships
When it comes to overcoming setbacks, the role of understanding mentors cannot be overstated. These mentors might be professors who genuinely enjoy assisting students. Gathering input from fellow students about these

individuals is a valuable practice. Additionally, if accessible, professional counselors can offer their guidance. Sharing your challenges with supportive family members consistently can be remarkably advantageous.

Similarly, cultivating a circle of optimistic friends can have an immensely positive impact. As mentioned earlier, research underscores that your G.P.A. tends to align with the average G.P.A. of the friends you regularly associate with. The value of these individuals extends beyond the present moment; they play a pivotal role in preparing you for a more promising future by fostering a positive outlook. It's important to recognize that you can change your circle of friends whenever necessary for your well-being.

The Role of Effective Reading

Numerous renowned individuals, such as Benjamin Franklin and Abraham Lincoln, attribute their accomplishments to their extensive reading habits. Reading inspirational books has even been credited with averting instances of suicidal impulses. To initiate your exploration, the references listed at the end of this book serve as an excellent starting point. If time constraints hinder you from delving into complete books before gauging your interest, a valuable approach involves perusing summaries or book abstracts accessible online. You can find abstracts for nearly three dozen exceptional books on my webpage titled "Joyful Living" (https://web.iitd.ac.in/~prb/). Many students have reaped the benefits of these resources.

Overcoming Suicidal Urges

The reasons behind contemplating suicide are intricate and diverse. Nonetheless, some common factors include the inability to cope with bullying, relationship breakdowns, academic underperformance, failure in competitive exams, struggle to secure employment, severe financial woes, and family disharmony.

While some students sink into depression due to prolonged feelings of failure and contemplate suicide after prolonged distress, others experience sudden, intense urges following a setback.

It's worth noting that while introverts are more susceptible to such feelings, some extroverts and successful have fallen victim to them.

The fear of pain while committing suicide or the thought of "What afterlife could be after this?" often prevents many from taking such a drastic step.

William James, the father of Modern American Psychology, was born into a wealthy and influential family. He suffered from many serious health problems from a young age. He was considered a black sheep in the family.

He was very depressed and one day decided to end his life. However, around that time, he chanced to read an essay by philosopher John Pierce. He was so impressed by it that he decided to experiment. In his diary, he wrote that he would spend one year believing he was 100 % responsible for everything that occurred in his life, no matter what. During this period, he would do everything he could to change his circumstances, no matter the likelihood of failure. If nothing improved that year, then it would be apparent that he was truly powerless to the circumstances around him, and then he would take his own life.

William James' life turned around significantly after this, and he expressed his gratitude to the author for the same.

As previously highlighted in this book, every life holds value. Yet, the primary driver of suicidal tendencies is often a lack of self-love, leading to diminished self-esteem. Practicing self-love consistently can serve as a preventive measure against these tendencies.

Research consistently demonstrates that the elements of Happiness Practice discussed in this book enhance emotional intelligence, thus boosting resilience in the face of challenges.

Beliefs and values shape our mental framework. Therefore, fostering self-awareness of these aspects and working to transform them into healthy ones is crucial. The stigma associated with failure largely stems from misguided mental conditioning.

Remember, every situation imaginable has been confronted and surmounted by someone in the past.

The sense of stigma is a construct of the ego. The book delves into how this construct fosters insecurity through comparison. Perceptions of events often hold more significance than reality, underscoring the importance of cultivating a constructive perspective. It's essential not to downplay a situation, yet also avoid magnifying it.

One widely effective strategy is maintaining a healthy dialogue with a higher power, or God, you believe in. This power doesn't necessarily eliminate challenges but shifts your outlook and provides the strength and wisdom to manage them. Acceptance of the situation and surrendering to a higher power greatly assists in reducing emotional turmoil.

Another immensely helpful approach is regularly journaling about painful experiences, especially during heightened distress. Developing the habit of releasing pent-up emotions onto paper or a digital platform diminishes their intensity significantly.

Seeking assistance from professional counselors, supportive faculty members, or online support groups has spared numerous lives from potential suicide.

We have found a Flower Remedy, "Rescue Remedy," very

effective in overcoming a feeling of intense trauma. It is important to consult psychiatrists and take the prescribed medicines.

Real Life Experiences

Following are the stories of individuals who have bounced back from various failures. As mentioned earlier, the names of the persons have been changed to protect their identities.

Students Wanting to Change Institute

During a personal counseling session, I had the opportunity to meet two first-year B. Tech students who expressed their dissatisfaction with the current institute and their desire to study at an Ivy League university in the U.S.A. One of them had an impressive ranking within the top ten admissions and was pursuing Computer Science Engineering, one of the most sought-after disciplines. The other student was equally talented, majoring in Electrical Engineering, another highly regarded field of study.

As I listened attentively to their concerns and understood their challenges, I realized that their unhappiness stemmed from internal factors rather than external circumstances. I earnestly conveyed to them that they might still experience discontent unless they addressed these inner issues, regardless of which institute they attended. Recognizing this truth, I suggested that it might be wiser for them to focus on resolving these internal struggles while they were still at their current institute and consider pursuing their dream of attending top-notch institutes for their Graduate studies.

Thankfully, they grasped the logic behind this advice and decided to stay back. As a result of their determination and efforts, they not only performed well academically but also found a sense of contentment and fulfilment in their journey.

Overcoming Depression

Harshit Gupta, a B. Tech student from the Computer Science Department, initially achieved an impressive C.G.P.A. of 9+ in his first year. However, his performance began to decline in the second year. Fearing disappointing his parents, he chose to conceal his struggles from them. Being an introvert, he found coping with the mounting stress challenging, eventually spiraling into depression. Consequently, his academic performance suffered even further. It reached a breaking point where he could no longer manage independently, prompting him to confide in his understanding parents. Seeking professional help, Harshit consulted a psychiatrist who prescribed medication. As a result, he had to take a semester off from his studies.

Harshit publicly shared his personal story, emphasizing that frequent communication with his parents about his well-being was the most significant factor in his recovery. He specifically highlighted the transformative impact of regular yoga and meditation practices on his overall state of mind. These interventions played a pivotal role in improving his mental health and academic performance. Today, he finds happiness and fulfillment in a top multinational company job.

Harshit's journey is a testament to the importance of seeking support from loved ones and mental health professionals when faced with depression. By openly addressing his struggles and embracing holistic practices, he rebuilt his well-being and successfully navigated his academic and professional life.

Overcoming Severe Odds

Chirag, a final-year B. Tech student, approached me seeking

counseling. He revealed that he had only accumulated around 35% of the credits required for graduation. He acknowledged how his past habits had affected his academic progress but assured me of his newfound seriousness. He sought my guidance on how to improve his situation. Chirag mentioned that he had taken up jogging every morning, which instilled a sense of enthusiasm within him. Upon assessing his credit score, I quickly calculated whether he could graduate within the maximum allowed timeframe for his degree.

I advised him to attend classes regularly, be on the front bench, and study more effectively. I also asked him to approach teachers and T.A.s frequently to clarify doubts. Considering his previous track record, my expectations were not particularly high. However, Chirag pleasantly surprised me by successfully passing all the courses he had registered for. This accomplishment fuelled his ambition, and he strongly desired to register for more courses next semester. However, I cautioned him about the risk of overburdening himself and potentially facing failure again due to an excessive workload. Ultimately, he graduated within the allotted time by maintaining a balanced approach.

Chirag's journey is a testament to the power of determination and making positive changes. Despite facing significant challenges, he managed to turn his academic situation around and achieve his degree goal.

Bouncing Back from Low Performance in the First Year

The transition to the I.I.T. environment can be challenging for many students, leading to a drastic decline in their G.P.A. during the first year. Hamid found himself in a similar situation, feeling hopeless about his prospects of improving his C.G.P.A. to a level that would secure a good job. To enhance his CV, he considered taking up extracurricular activities. However, most students in a similar predicament choose activities that do not contribute to their objectives or academics.

In contrast, Hamid made a different choice. He decided to engage in N.S.S. (National Service Scheme) activities. Fortunately for him, his fellow students involved in N.S.S. had positive attitudes and excelled academically. Their influence transformed Hamid's outlook, instilling a positive approach in his life. Despite dedicating less time to his studies due to his involvement in N.S.S. activities, Hamid significantly improved his C.G.P.A. This illustrates the profound impact of the group one interacts with on their attitude and qualities.

The Power of Self-Study

Following the JEE results, Aman pursued Mining Engineering at I.I.T. B.H.U., a field he wasn't particularly passionate about. Nevertheless, he managed to complete the program with a decent C.G.P.A. Subsequently, he embarked on a year of independent study, focusing on computer-related courses. Additionally, he gained practical experience by working in a start-up. Building on this foundation, he pursued an M.S. in abroad in Computer Science. Today, he is content with his position at Facebook. What makes his journey even more remarkable is that despite having a father who was an I.I.T. professor and could have guided him, Aman chose the self-study path. However, this transition was far from smooth, as he encountered numerous setbacks before finally achieving success.

Overcoming Stress in an Ivy League Institute

Shubhangi, a silver medallist graduate from I.I.T., embarked on her Ph.D. journey at an Ivy League university. During her first semester, she enrolled in challenging courses, believing that her background would be advantageous. However, she soon discovered that her classmates possessed exceptional intelligence and a stronger foundation and were significantly ahead of her in these subjects. Initially, Shubhangi struggled academically, plagued by the fear of failure, which caused tremendous stress. Aware of my student counseling initiative from our previous association at I.I.T. Delhi, she sought my guidance for navigating this daunting situation.

I gave her the usual advice: to cease comparing herself to others, focus on the present moment, and dedicate her efforts to daily tasks to the best of her ability. Moreover, I encouraged her to recall her past accomplishments and relish her confidence, assuring her that she could handle the workload at the Ivy League Institute. Shubhangi heeded my advice, and by the end of the semester, she reported back to me with great satisfaction, revealing that she had performed exceptionally well. From that point forward, she never looked back.

Shubhangi's story exemplifies the power of resilience and adopting a positive mindset when faced with challenges in a highly competitive academic environment. She overcame the initial stress by letting go of comparisons, staying focused, and drawing confidence from past achievements and thrived in her Ph.D. studies. Her journey inspires others to navigate similar circumstances, reminding them of their strengths and potential for success.

Bouncing Back Late

Gopal was a Textile engineering 4th year student. He did not do well academically in the first five semesters, and his C.G.P.A. was around 6.5. He suddenly realized that his future was bleak unless he did something drastic. He met a professor he admired for his research and convinced him about his serious intent to work hard. He asked for a project that could result in a publication. The Professor believed him and encouraged him, providing all the support. He did so well in that project that he got a summer internship with financial support from a Hong Kong university. He also got a Ph.D. position at the same university because of his good work, which impressed his supervisor.

Incredible Transformation

Anmol Singh, a dual-degree student from I.I.T. Delhi, experienced a remarkable turnaround during his 5th semester. He found himself grappling with a multitude of challenges, including academic struggles, financial difficulties, and family issues. Seeking guidance on how to improve his life, he turned to me for advice.

I suggested that Anmol embrace his past without holding onto bitterness and redirect his focus away from worrying about the uncertain future. I recommended reading my webpage articles, and to my delight, Anmol was the only student who not only read them but also engaged in detailed discussions with me.

In the early stages of our interactions, Anmol shared a fascinating experience regarding his performance in two courses. He had initially believed that his old study habits would suffice for an easier course. Still, he decided to experiment with the study tips from my articles in a more challenging one. Surprisingly, he performed below expectations in the former and exceeded them in the latter. Convinced of the effectiveness of the new approach, Anmol began implementing many of the strategies outlined in my articles.

He delved into self-help literature, adopted positive self-talk, and practiced visualization techniques. As a result, his academic performance improved significantly. Moreover, he embarked on two impactful projects—one focused on social empowerment for rural communities and another on early disease diagnostics using A.I. tools. Although his B. Tech C.G.P.A. remained below seven due to subpar grades in the first two years, his master's part of the dual degree saw his C.G.P.A. soar close to 10.

Anmol's accomplishments extended beyond academia. He secured funding for both of his projects and obtained a faculty mentor. Additionally, he achieved financial stability through a lucrative part-time job opportunity. When he shared these achievements with me, Anmol radiated happiness; his life had undergone a profound transformation, and he expressed great confidence in his prospects.

Relationship Failure

Handling failure in relationships, especially romantic ones, can be challenging for many students. In some cases, it has even led to tragic outcomes like suicide. While there's nothing wrong with having relationships, it's essential to understand that they involve mutual chemistry. Therefore, it's implicit that both individuals can end the relationship if further progress is impossible at any stage. Trying to cling to a relationship at any cost can be disastrous and a sign of insecurity. Clear communication, mutual understanding of expectations, and open conversations are vital during the exploration of a relationship. After moving on from a relationship that didn't work, both individuals can seek new relationships without feeling guilty.

Some students consider themselves failures if they are not in a relationship. They might envy those who are in relationships. They start finding faults within themselves, which can lead to a loss of self-esteem. Many students believe a lack of specific physical, intellectual, or financial attributes holds them back. However, my extensive experience has convinced me that none of these factors should hold you back if you strive to be the best version of yourself. When you focus on believing in giving more than receiving in a relationship, you naturally exude peace, warmth, and happiness. Such individuals are in high demand in this self-centered world. When you prioritize personal growth and become genuinely caring, you won't have to chase after relationships; suitable individuals will be drawn to you.

Bouncing Back from Emotional Turmoil after a Breakup

An intelligent student, Sandhya experienced a romantic relationship during her first year at I.I.T. Unfortunately, this relationship caused her to neglect her studies. Her boyfriend ended their relationship in her second year and became involved with someone else. Sandhya felt humiliated and believed that her classmates were mocking her. Her self-esteem plummeted, and she lost interest in her academic pursuits. She found herself attending failed courses alongside her juniors, perceiving their judgment of her as a weak student. This led to a state of deep sadness and depression. For a prolonged period, she kept her situation hidden from her parents. Desperate to prove her worth to her ex-boyfriend and the world, she reached a point where she even contemplated suicide. Seeking guidance, she approached me to share her story.

I attentively listened to her narrative and endeavoured to convince her of the value of her life. I assured her that people are so consumed by their concerns that they rarely take notice of others, let alone pity them. I explained that her belief that she was being judged and her ensuing suffering resulted from her distorted thinking. I advised her to release the need to prove herself to the world, as this would only perpetuate her anguish. Instead, I encouraged her to pursue her passions wholeheartedly because she loved doing so. I also emphasized the importance of not giving up on relationships due to one unfortunate experience. To illustrate this, I shared stories of a courageous woman who, despite experiencing two divorces, ultimately found a deeply fulfilling relationship on her third attempt.

Furthermore, I suggested that Sandhya read books by Kamal Ravikant and Louise Hay. She followed my guidance and gradually regained her enthusiasm. In hindsight, Sandhya recognized how practicing self-love transformed her life. She learned to embrace her worth and rebuild her inner strength.

Maintaining a Positive Attitude After Low Performance in a Difficult Course

Angela Duckworth, the famous author of "Grit," had enrolled in a difficult Neurobiology course in her first year of college. It was tough for her because she lacked some background. She started panicking and felt that she might fail in that course. Hence, she could not concentrate on her studies and did poorly in the first quiz. The instructor warned her that she could fail and advised her to withdraw from the course. She did poorly in the second quiz as well, and the warning from the instructor was sterner. There was panic, but her self-talk was still positive. She felt she could still do well. She tried harder and took all possible help from teaching assistants. She asked for extra work, practiced solving tougher problems under time pressure, mimicked exam conditions, and produced flawless performance. She knew her nerves could be a problem and decided to attain a level of mastery in the course preparation so that nothing could surprise her. Finally, she got a 'B' in the course.

My wife also faced a similar situation in I.I.T. Bombay when she registered for a typical course as a Pre-Ph.D. student. Since the system was completely new, she got very low marks in her first test, which panicked her, and she thought she might fail the course. However, her elder brother trusted her inherent capability and assured her she would get an "A." It appeared absurd at that time. But nothing works as trust shown by the person whom you value, just like anything. He just sowed the seeds of fierce struggle and gave her tips on how to proceed. She became very calm and met the instructor, who was initially reluctant to meet. She could convince him that although she had not done well in the first test, she was serious about doing well and was prepared to work hard to any extent. She asked him to suggest the best resources for studying that course and asked about the nature of general questions in future tests and what kind of answers were expected for the best grade. She also looked at the answer books of those who had done well in the first test to know the difference in their way of answering questions. Eventually, she got an "A" grade, which surprised everyone. It exemplified self-confidence, perseverance, and going the extra mile to fetch the result.

Drug De-addiction

The issue of drug addiction has become a major concern for parents of the younger generation. We know the disastrous consequences drugs can have on health and academic performance. Once you fall into the trap of addiction, breaking free becomes difficult. Therefore, prevention is always better than cure. It's easy to be lured into the world of drugs if you're not careful. Addicts may try to mix drugs into drinks or persuade you to try a small dose to convince you that it's fun and harmless. However, once you start, your body will demand more and more. The best approach is to tactfully distance yourself from individuals involved in drugs as soon as you suspect their activities. You must also learn to be firm and say "No" to drugs. If you inadvertently find yourself trapped in drug addiction and experience cravings, it's essential to confide in your parents and seek guidance from counselors. The earlier you act, the better. Because of this danger, support groups on academic campuses are dedicated to helping those in need.

De-addiction from Devices and social media

In today's modern world, many of us have fallen victim to the ever-expanding threat of addiction to devices like phones, iPads, laptops, and social media platforms. Countless dollars are invested by device manufacturers, gaming companies, and social media giants to keep us hooked. Due to their pervasive nature and low costs, this addiction is potentially far more dangerous than drug addiction. It is predicted that successful individuals of the future will not necessarily be the most talented but rather those who combine their talents and wisdom to use devices and social media for their benefit without becoming slaves to them. Tips on how to achieve this balance have already been discussed elsewhere.

Breaking Free from Online Gambling

Alok and a couple of his friends found themselves trapped in online gambling. As students at I.I.T., they believed they could outsmart the system and strike it rich. Despite his addiction, Alok managed to maintain a 7+ C.G.P.A. in his final year. However, he lost so much money that he couldn't afford to pay his hostel dues for several months, and he even received an eviction notice. On top of that, his sister's wedding was just around the corner. Being from a middle-class family, he couldn't bring himself to confess his situation to his parents. His future career was hanging by a thread, with placement interviews approaching in a few months.

At this critical stage, Alok sought counseling from me. He admitted to trying to quit gambling, but the urge to recoup his losses always pulled him back in. I explained to him how these gambling agencies invested millions of dollars in developing a system that entices people with occasional small wins. Still, in the long run, it leads to significant losses. This revelation convinced him to steer clear of gambling in the future.

However, the challenge remained: how could he gather enough money to pay his hostel dues? In a show of support, I offered him some assistance, suggesting he could pay me back once he secured a job. Alok was deeply moved by my trust in him but declined the offer. Instead, he managed to get help from some senior friends who were already employed.

After a few months passed, Alok stopped me one day after my class with a radiant smile. He happily shared the news that he had landed a good banking job. I congratulated him on his success, feeling joyous that his promising career was back on track.

• • •

CHAPTER XVIII

Preparing for the Future

"Good fortune is what happens when opportunity meets with planning." - Thomas Edison.

When you embark on your academic journey in college, it's ideal to start thinking about the future right from your first year. Long-term planning is a valuable life skill that can lead to the best outcomes. The best part is that planning can be enjoyable and exciting. Your plans will naturally evolve as you gain maturity and wisdom through various experiences. This allows you to align your strengths and aspirations, creating a harmonious path. The advantage of a long time frame is that it enables you to prepare gradually and steadily without unnecessary stress. However, it's important to remember that achieving your top priority is never guaranteed, so it's wise to have fallback options by creating a priority list.

To prepare for the future, seeking information from multiple sources, especially the internet, is essential. However, don't overlook the valuable insights of happy and accomplished individuals in your field of interest. Developing the skill of seeking help from others is crucial for personal growth. Learning to ask the right questions is equally important. You can dedicate some time on weekends and holidays to this pursuit, and during winter and summer breaks, you can delve deeper into the process. A common mistake made by those who engage in such activities is failing to record the acquired information in a journal, whether in digital or physical form, along with the date. This journal becomes a precious resource for your future endeavors.

Even if you strongly prefer specific career options, exploring other possibilities is wise. Your earlier preferences may have been based on limited information and a relatively immature and less wise perspective. Maintaining an open mind allows room for your preferences to change and evolve.

Many students decide about their post-graduation plans in their first year of college. While clarity is not inherently wrong, their choices based on their academic pursuits can create problems. For instance, students who intend to pursue an M.B.A., appear for Civil Services exams, or choose consulting or finance jobs often feel that their core subjects (engineering or science) are irrelevant to their future aspirations. Consequently, they may focus solely on obtaining decent grades in these courses, neglecting the value of learning. However, this attitude is risky because, as mentioned earlier, your choices can change as you progress through your degree program, acquiring additional information and wisdom.

Moreover, changes in the national and global economy, government policies, and other market factors can sometimes render your initial choices less attractive than alternative paths. Many alumni have cautioned against making such mistakes. I've personally witnessed students who, despite two attempts, failed to clear the civil services exam and had to rely on their technical knowledge to secure jobs in their core sectors. Similarly, those who seek opportunities abroad by pursuing a master's degree may encounter significant obstacles due to policy changes in their desired countries.

When considering job opportunities, many students tend to focus primarily on hefty pay packages rather than factors like learning potential, growth prospects, and overall happiness. However, even if you land a high-paying job that doesn't bring you joy, your life will be filled with unhappiness. Your potential for improvement is likely to be stifled in such a position. On the other hand, if you find a lower-paying job that you genuinely enjoy, you'll experience happiness while continuously enhancing your skills. This approach contributes to your future success and has a cumulative effect on your overall well-being, positively impacting your relationships with friends and family.

As you approach the job interviews, you'll clearly understand your C.G.P.A. and the companies for which you are eligible. Securing top-tier jobs involves several selection stages, such as aptitude tests, technical tests, elaborate interviews, and group discussions for managerial positions. Large-scale recruiters typically combine aptitude and technical tests, followed by a short interview.

While preparing for your chosen aspiration or job, it's important to identify the required skill sets and develop them gradually and systematically. Depending on your field, this may involve grasping the basic concepts, honing your problem-solving abilities, acquiring programming skills, or becoming proficient in using relevant instruments and software packages. Documenting key points and insights into these skills will prove immensely helpful, particularly during the demanding final year. It's worth noting that success in exams like GRE, C.A.T., G.A.T.E., and U.P.S.C. in your final year doesn't necessarily depend on innate brilliance but rather on long-term preparation, as mentioned earlier.

Even if you are interested in pursuing higher studies, appearing for U.P.S.C. exams, or starting a business, it's still advisable to participate in campus interviews. This experience provides invaluable exposure at no cost.

When considering further studies, such as pursuing an M.S. or an M.B.A., it's important to evaluate long-term opportunities and not rush into a decision. Remember, you'll be working for a considerable duration, so choosing the right path is crucial. However, there can also be benefits to working for a few years before pursuing higher education. This period allows for personal growth, gaining maturity, and developing a broader perspective on the job market, ultimately leading to a better-informed specialization selection. For example, my younger son opted to work for a year, gaining wisdom and experience before pursuing an M.S. at C.M.U. U.S.A.

While job hunting, many factors, such as market conditions, are beyond your control. Therefore, adopting the serenity principle and focusing on what you can do with a positive and content mindset is important. Embrace the process, enjoy the preparation, and avoid becoming desperate for immediate results. This approach reduces stress, enhances the joy of the journey, and improves your overall efficiency.

When determining the types of employers, you're targeting and why, it's crucial to be realistic and practical. Once you've reasoned through your choices, the process becomes more manageable. Gather information about the job profile and interview format from the employment organization and other sources, such as alumni working in similar positions. Contact the organization directly and inquire about the specific requirements and expectations. This will provide valuable insights into the interview process and what the company is looking for in potential candidates.

Preparing for Interviews

Once you understand the preparation and time needed, create a comprehensive action plan that aligns with your regular semester activities. This plan should include weekly and daily tasks, ensuring it integrates smoothly with your schedule.

Interview preparation is usually extensive, covering various subjects and courses you have studied. The sheer volume of resources to study can feel overwhelming, but there's no need to be intimidated. Instead, approach it with a smart, systematic, persevering, and efficient mindset. During interviews or exams, not all courses will be equally relevant. Before the interview, you won't have time to revisit all the books and detailed notes. Keeping concise notes from the important courses you've studied will be helpful. Working on your preparation over the long term is beneficial to avoid last-minute stress. Remember that interviewers are more interested in assessing your understanding of basic concepts and ability to apply logic than expecting you to memorize everything. They want to gauge your aptitude, confidence, and problem-solving skills in real-world scenarios. If you encounter a question for which you don't have an exact answer, focus on demonstrating your logical thinking and ability to conclude when given hints or prompts.

You may have to undergo aptitude and technical tests. When preparing for such entrance or qualifying tests, it's highly recommended to practice time-bound mock tests specifically tailored to interview scenarios. Despite aptitude being considered a latent quality, mock tests are still valuable because they familiarize you with the questions and reduce stress during the test. Moreover, mock tests help develop essential time management skills, which are crucial for success in these tests.

In many cases, interviewers intentionally pose open-ended questions without a specific answer. They do this to assess your confidence and logic in tackling such problems, as real-life situations often involve ambiguous scenarios. Be prepared to introduce yourself and explain why the company should hire you. Although the exact time given for this may vary, you can seek reasonable estimates from seniors who have previously undergone similar interview processes. It's advisable to have bullet points of self-introduction that can be expanded upon depending on the time available.

Just as you take care of your energy needs during your regular studies, it's important to prioritize your well-being and maintain a positive frame of mind throughout the interview preparation process. On the day of the interview, avoid excessive last-minute preparation. Instead, focus on reviewing general strategies for facing interviews. Remain relaxed, peaceful, and confident; these qualities will help you perform at your best.

Facing the Interview

While waiting for your turn in the outside hall, there are several techniques you can employ to reduce stress. In your mind, thank the organization for granting you the interview opportunity and wish them success in their business endeavors. Look at other candidates with a smile and wish them well in finding good jobs. Take a moment to pray for strength, wisdom, and a harmonious interview. If needed, practice deep breathing exercises.

During the interview, you will be evaluated based on your technical knowledge, aptitude, and personality. This assessment creates a crucial first impression. Good body language and maintaining eye contact are essential. When you enter the interview hall, greet the committee members with a pleasant "good morning" or appropriate greetings based on the time of the interview. As you take your seat, keep your body relaxed. Avoid sitting on the edge of the chair and rest your arms on the chair while maintaining an upright posture that isn't too rigid. Keep your feet steady and maintain a slight smile throughout the interview. When the chairman introduces you to the experts, make eye contact with each one and silently wish them well. Additionally, take a moment to pray for a harmonious interview. These actions take minimal time but can significantly contribute to maintaining a relaxed state.

The interview committee chairperson may ask you to introduce yourself and explain how you can contribute to their organization. Sticking to your prepared plan and ensuring you cover all important points is best. At this stage, detailed information is not always necessary. In any case, the experts can request further clarification if needed. When the questions begin, maintain eye contact with the expert, take a deep breath, and carefully understand the question. Avoid rushing to answer immediately. If the question is unclear, don't hesitate to seek clarification. The experts appreciate your willingness to ask for clarification, giving you additional seconds to formulate an answer. Make a peaceful decision on whether you can answer the question; if you cannot, politely inform them that you don't know the answer. Most of the time, the experts appreciate your honesty and may provide hints to see if you can logically extend your reasoning. If you can, proceed slowly. If not, don't waste time and move on to other questions you can answer. Remember, the time allocated per candidate is fixed, and by doing this, you create more opportunities for questions you can confidently address.

Almost every candidate will face questions they can't answer. Take a few deep breaths in such moments and pray for inner peace. This is crucial because the interview process can be highly stressful without these practices. Remember that the interview explores finding the best match between their requirements and your capabilities. It may not work out because many factors are beyond your control. The entire interview process is imperfect, and peacefully accepting this is important. Remember that it's not a life-or-death situation. You have other options, and with the right attitude and effort, you will find the match mentioned earlier.

The Allure of Start-ups

Many of you may be drawn to the success stories of young professionals who struck it rich through start-ups. While there's nothing wrong with aspiring to this, it's important to grasp a few concepts before diving headlong into this realm. First and foremost your desires and your abilities must be aligned. Understanding market opportunities and whether your idea addresses a specific need while also being economically feasible is crucial. Often, crafting and executing such ideas requires a collaborative effort.

Furthermore, it would help if you comprehended the complete sequence of steps leading from the initial idea to a profitable venture. Notably, some distinguished I.I.T. alumni have emphasized that while the intellectual foundation is vital, diverse management skills encompassing finance and marketing play an equally significant role. This is a big reason why the success rate of start-ups remains under 5%. Venturing into this domain involves a high-risk, high-reward scenario. Therefore, it might not be your best path unless you're emotionally and financially prepared for such an endeavor.

Additionally, even if you're determined to pursue this path, it's wise to have backup options ready, given the potential risks of failure mentioned earlier. Striving for balance in all aspects of your life is paramount. This entails making a wide-ranging selection of courses and not allocating excessive time to your start-up idea to the detriment of your academic pursuits. For more guidance on this matter, you can turn to the Time Management chapter for valuable insights.

Suggestions for Those Who Can't Secure a Good Campus Job

If you find yourself ineligible for good jobs due to a low C.G.P.A. or if you're not selected in interviews, it's not the end of your career. Consider what steps you can take instead of dwelling on what has happened.

Numerous individuals have achieved great success after experiencing initial setbacks. Jack Ma is one such example, having faced multiple failures on his path to success.

You may consider appearing for exams like G.R.E., G.M.A.T., GATE, J.A.M., or N.E.T. to improve your academic profile and become eligible for P.S.U. jobs. This option is particularly beneficial for students from lower-ranked colleges. For those aspiring for government jobs, appearing for the U.P.S.C. exam is advisable. If feasible, joining reputable coaching classes for these exams can be helpful. However, if that's impossible, collect coaching material and practice exam papers independently. Be prepared to dedicate significant time and effort over a year if you're serious about securing a better future.

Another valuable option is to seek out projects with esteemed institutions like I.I.T. These institutions often have high-value research and development projects that require additional manpower. You may need to approach faculty members, express your willingness to work hard and convince them of your capabilities and dedication. Be prepared to work without immediate monetary compensation initially, as this can help demonstrate your sincerity and commitment.

Overall, various elegant ways exist to achieve your goals without losing hope and compromising your peace of mind. There is enough sunshine mixed with small rains for everybody to complete this serene journey called life.

• • •

References

1. Happier, Tal Ben-Shahar, McGraw Hill, 2008
2. Happiness Advantage, Shawn Achor, Virgin Books, 2011
3. Search Inside Yourself, Chade-Meng Tan, Thorson's, Harper Collins, 2013
4. Joy On Demand, Chade-Meng Tan, Harper One, Harper Collins, 2016
5. Awaken the Giant Within, Anthony Robbins, Pocketbooks, Simon Schuster, 2001
6. Man's Search for Meaning, Viktor Frankl, Beacon Press, 1959
7. Autobiography of Benjamin Franklin, Fingerprint Classics, 2018
8. Love Yourself as If Your Life Depends on It, Kamal Ravikant, HQ, 2020
9. You Can Heal Your Life, Louise Hay, Hay House, 2008
10. Six Pillars of Self-Esteem, Nathaniel Branden, Rhus, 1995
11. Power of Subconscious Mind, Joseph Murphy, Bantam Books, 2001
12. The Power of Now, Eckhart Tolle, Yogi impressions, 2010
13. The Untethered Soul, Michael A. Singer, Generic, 2020
14. Choose the Life You Want, Tal Ben-Shahar, The Experiment LLC, 2017
15. The Subtle Art of Not Giving a Fuck, Mark Manson, Harper One, 2016
16. Happiness Unlimited, Sister Shivani in conversation with Suresh Oberoi, Third Eye, Manjul Publishing House, 2015

17. Think Like a Monk, Jay Shetty, Thorson's, 2020

18. The Power of Positive Thinking, Norman Vincent Peale, Ballantine Books, New York, 1982

19. A Whole New Life, Lucia Giovannini, Hay House, 2016

20. The Headspace Guide to Mindfulness and Meditation, Andy Puddicombe, Hodder and Stoughton, 2011

21. Before Happiness, Shawn Achor, Virgin Books, 2013

22. Winning Habits, B. P. Bam, Pearson, 2009

23. Grit, Angela Duckworth, Scribner Book Company, 2016

24. The Science of Prayer, The Wall Street Journal, May 2020

25. The Power of Affirmations and Their Secret to Success, Louise Stapely, Amazon, January 2014

26. ,The Upward Spiral, Alex Corb, January 2014, New Harbinger, 2015

27. The Little Book of Gratitude, Robert A. Emmons, Gaia Books, Octopus Publishing, 2016

28. The Magic, Rhonda Byrne, Simon & Schuster, 2012

29. Atomic Habits, James Clear, Avery, 2018

30. Love, Medicines and Miracles, Bernie Siegel, Harper Collins, 1986

Acknowledgments

I want to express my gratitude to the invaluable influences that have shaped this book. The teachings of my revered Guru, Shri Bramhachaitanya Gondavlekar Maharaj (1845-1913), have profoundly impacted my professional and personal journey. I was struck by the resonance between his wisdom and the themes I found in numerous self-help books. His central message, emphasizing the recognition of divinity in all aspects of our surroundings, not just within humanity but throughout the entire environment, has been instrumental in guiding my path. His teachings on Mantra meditation, gratitude, helping others, mindfulness, being unburdened by past grievances or future anxieties, and giving our very best in all our pursuits have provided the foundational principles of this book.

In 2014, Mr. Shubham Bharadwaj, a final-year Electrical Engineering student, initiated discussions with me about his grasp of various spiritual concepts. Upon discovering my notes on spiritual learning and personal abstracts from self-help books, he passionately encouraged me to share my insights with the student community. His unwavering support led to my webpage, housing these articles. Subsequently, Dr. Arjun Tyagi and Mr. Bevin, from the Department of Energy Studies, devoted their efforts to enhancing and maintaining the webpage. However, as time advanced, I felt the constraints of the webpage format and began contemplating the idea of expanding my articles into a comprehensive book.

Over nearly five years, I had the privilege of imparting the content of these articles to numerous groups of first-year students enrolled in a Values and Ethics-based course at I.I.T. Delhi. The feedback from these students was overwhelmingly positive, and it was during this time that I also had the opportunity to share my ideas through a multitude of lectures conducted for diverse student audiences.

During individual counseling sessions, I was fortunate to engage with countless students, from the first year of undergraduate studies to the ones pursuing Ph.D. degrees. These sessions gave me valuable insights into the spectrum of problems they faced.

Authors of many self-help books have influenced the contents of this book. Prominent among them are the Late Rev Norman Vincent Peale, Stephen Covey, Anthony Robbins, Shawn Achor, Chade Meng-Tan, and Tal-Ben Shahar.

While I have made earnest efforts, I know mistakes and oversights may still linger on these pages concerning acknowledgments. I am open to receiving corrections or omissions that deserve rectification and commit to making the necessary amendments.

My heartfelt appreciation goes to my wife, Jayashree, a superannuated Professor at I.I.T. Delhi, who has been my unwavering support and strength throughout my endeavors. She consistently buoyed my spirits when I contemplated abandoning this book, and her contributions extended to comprehensive book review and editing. My children, Chaitanya and Chinmay, along with my daughters-in-law, Bhawna and Snigdha, were of immense help in ensuring my enthusiasm remained unwavering. Chinmay provided substantial reviews which motivated me to improve.

I am grateful for Dr. S.A. Khaparde, former Professor at I.I.T. Bombay, who introduced me to the spiritual path of our Guru and was of continuous help throughout this journey.

I sincerely appreciate Prof. S.G. Deshmukh, from I.I.T. Delhi, and the former Director of I.I.I.T.M. Gwalior, who consistently encouraged my student engagements. He was kind enough to review the book and provide very insightful comments for its improvement.

I sincerely appreciate Shubham Bharadwaj's extensive book review.

Dr. Umesh Marathe, Reasearch Associate, Oak Ridge National Laboratory, USA, has been a tremendous help for many years in many ways.

I am grateful to Mr. Devendra Bantpelliwar of Media Research and Development Pvt Ltd., who lent their invaluable assistance in designing the book cover.

I extend my heartfelt thanks to the Notion Press team for their support in facilitating the publication of this book.

Finally, I extend my gratitude to you, the reader, for investing your precious time and resources in exploring the contents of this book. Your feedback will be invaluable in enhancing the substance of this work.

www.ingramcontent.com/pod-product-compliance
Lightning Source LLC
Chambersburg PA
CBHW041309120726
48005CB00014B/1932